BEST OF
BLOCK

by MISSOURI STAR QUILT CO.

EXECUTIVE EDITOR
Natalie Earnheart

CREATIVE TEAM
Jenny Doan, Natalie Earnheart, Christine Ricks, Tyler MacBeth, Mike Brunner, Lauren Dorton, Jennifer Dowling, Dustin Weant, Jessica Toye, Kimberly Forman, Denise Lane

EDITORS & COPYWRITERS
Nichole Spravzoff, Camille Maddox, David Litherland, Julie Barber-Arutyunyan

SEWIST TEAM
Jenny Doan, Natalie Earnheart, Courtenay Hughes, Carol Henderson, Janice Richardson, Aislinn Earnheart, Janet Yamamoto, Denise Lane

PRINTING COORDINATOR
Rob Stoebener

PRINTING SERVICES
Walsworth Print Group
803 South Missouri
Marceline, MO 64658

CONTACT US
Missouri Star Quilt Company
114 N Davis
Hamilton, MO 64644
888-571-1122
info@missouriquiltco.com

MISSOURI STAR
QUILT CO.

THE
BEST OF BLOCK

Best of BLOCK is like an album of Missouri Star's greatest hits. We just keep coming back to these gorgeous patterns time and time again, like our favorite songs. They're quilts that have challenged us, surprised us, and they've become favorites for a reason. Each one is unique and if you haven't tried one of them yet, we have a feeling you'll find a new favorite among them. We've gathered up groups of patterns specifically for 10″ squares, 5″ squares, and 2½″ strips to help you make the most of your time and we'll show you all the things these amazing precuts can do!

A note from Jenny

Dear Quilters,

Looking back over the past seven years of BLOCK Magazine has done my heart good. I love everything that we've done so far and I am incredibly proud of all the work that has gone into these heartfelt idea books. After creating over 52 quilts a year, there are bound to be a few favorites and this special issue is a collection of the very best we have to offer! If you're brand new to BLOCK or you've been a devoted subscriber for years, this issue is sure to inspire you. The inspiration never stops coming, so many of the classic Missouri Star quilts you know and love have been refreshed in brand new fabrics and we've also added some new projects, too!

Inside the pages of this big, beautiful book you'll definitely recognize a few familiar favorites, but we've tucked in plenty of surprises, too. Discover more about Missouri Star's very own quilting magazine and find yourself in love with quilting all over again with the Best of BLOCK.

Jenny

JENNY DOAN
MISSOURI STAR QUILT CO.

The Missouri Star Story

BUILDING A BUSINESS, BLOCK BY BLOCK

Starting a quilt company was never part of my life's plan. I've come to realize that plans are meant to change and I truly believe that life doesn't always turn out the way you imagine it—sometimes it's even better.

From the time I was young, I had planned on being a mother. That was my ultimate goal. And I was incredibly blessed with seven wonderful children. Children change you forever, and my family has done more to shape me and help me grow than any other influence in my life. It was my sweet children who came to me when times got hard and proposed a plan to help me and my husband have a retirement. It was my children who asked me to start teaching people to quilt online. And, even to this very day, my children continually challenge me to become the best version of myself.

As I look back over the years, our journey began with a single decision. We realized that staying in California wasn't going to be the best plan for our family. I rarely speak about this time in our lives, but it was incredibly difficult. Our son, Josh, had developed a lymphatic tumor. There were days I wasn't sure if he would survive and I thought sadness might overcome me. Somehow, we made it through, and Josh is completely fine today, but as a result, the medical bills nearly bankrupted us. We decided to make some changes to help our family grow and the time felt right to pack up and begin a new life across the country. We literally pulled out a map, pointed to a spot somewhere in the Midwest and said, "That's where we'll go!" It's clear to us now that this seemingly random choice wasn't random at all—I know that we were guided to the right place for us. And that's how we ended up in Hamilton, Missouri.

Like many small towns in America in the mid-2000s, Hamilton was struggling due to a downturn in the economy. More than a century before, it had been the hometown of successful entrepreneur James Cash Penney himself and later on he even put his 500th store right on the main street. But by the time we moved in, many of those beautiful old storefronts sat empty, including the JC Penney store. Nevertheless, it was a charming town filled with wonderful people and I was proud to call it home. We happily went about raising our children in Hamilton, but because work was scarce in town, for years my husband Ron traveled an

hour and a half each way to his job at the Kansas City Star newspaper. In 2008, we got the news that Ron lost his retirement because of the market crash. The newspaper industry was a sinking ship and people were being laid off monthly. It was a tough time for our family and we weren't sure what to do next.

That's when my daughter, Sarah, and my son, Alan, came to me with a plan to start a business that would help us with our retirement. It was a modest idea at first. They wanted to help me purchase a longarm quilting machine and run a family quilting business in one of the empty storefronts in town. Our very own quilt shop! The idea absolutely thrilled me. Before we moved to Missouri, I had been a seamstress and mainly sewed clothing, but soon after we moved, quilting quickly

That November, we went ahead with our plan and bought a longarm and a small brick building in town that was just minutes away from our house. We called our new business the "Missouri Star Quilt Company."

became a passion of mine when I took my very first quilting class. It was a quilt in a day class about the Log Cabin pattern held in Chillicothe at the Vo-tech school. And I've been quilting ever since!

That November, we went ahead with our plan and bought a longarm and a small brick building in town that was just minutes away from our house. We called our new business the "Missouri Star Quilt Company" and soon found that there weren't a lot of customers in a town of 1,500 people. Well, that didn't stop us! Thank goodness Alan didn't listen to me after all those years I told him to get off the computer because he then used his skills to set up the business online. He brought in a good friend, David Mifsud, who he had met during his time serving a mission for the Church of Jesus Christ of Latter-day Saints in Kiev, Ukraine. These

I still remember when Alan came to me back in early 2009 and asked me if I wanted to teach quilting tutorials online. I asked him, "What's a tutorial?"

two boys had always dreamed of going into business together and the time was right. With David's financial background and Alan's technical know-how, they were able to help start a successful online business, even in the midst of a financial crisis. I still consider this an actual miracle.

Sarah helped me run the shop in town and Alan and David went to work online. In the early days, we didn't sell much, but things changed after we took quilting to YouTube! I still remember when Alan came to me back in early 2009 and asked me if I wanted to teach quilting tutorials online. I asked him, "What's a tutorial?" He laughed a little and soon had me set up in front of a camera. Looking back on that first quilting tutorial, it's incredible to see how far Missouri Star has come! There I was, stitching with my home sewing machine and the iron I'd used for years, sitting down (because I'd broken my foot!), and teaching a simple 4-patch block using a jelly roll. I had no idea what the future held for our tiny company. Twelve short years later, many wonderful milestones have been reached thanks to your support and love of quilting.

Because I had a background in musical theater, I warmed up to being on camera so frequently and I really began to enjoy filming our weekly quilting tutorials. And, wouldn't you know? People wanted to buy the fabrics and notions we used to make our quilts. It was miraculous! All the things we showed in the videos went into the online shop and people bought them. The business began to make money and when we got our first actual paycheck,

we had to pinch ourselves! We spent very little money on advertising in the first few years and relied almost entirely on our own creativity to grow. Before long, our quilting tutorials became very popular on YouTube and we found out that Missouri Star was actually the largest quilting channel. That was just amazing to me. I couldn't imagine that hundreds of thousands of people wanted to watch me quilt, but they kept on watching and I am so grateful.

As new customers began to find us online, they wanted patterns to go along with our videos and they also wished they could order patterns and not have

them run out and go away forever. So, we started thinking and we decided to make our very own pattern book filled with original quilts and stories. Block Magazine began with this big idea and it has turned into one of our favorite things about Missouri Star.

Before we began publishing Block Magazine, we had been submitting quilt patterns to other magazines out there and paying them to publish our patterns. The challenge was, once that issue came out, it soon disappeared, along with our quilt pattern. Magazines were also declining in popularity because of the digital age and social media and many

...we have continued to publish Block Magazine every other month. After seven wonderful years, we don't anticipate stopping any time soon! Block continues to be a work of heart and we enjoy creating every single issue just for you.

were going out of business. So, we decided to make our own magazine that didn't rely on advertising and publish our own patterns instead of turning to outside sources. We had plenty of unpublished patterns from all our YouTube videos to start. A small team of three people began the magazine and created it entirely from scratch.

The very first issue of Block came out in February of 2013. It was a freezing cold day and the team was all huddled around a table in my old sewing studio where we used to film tutorials, finalizing Block before it went to press. There hadn't been much fanfare leading up to the day we announced Block would be published, but everyone sure seemed excited to hear it was coming out! Right away, we started to see all of our customers reacting to this news—and what a response it was! Since

then we have continued to publish Block Magazine every other month. After seven wonderful years, we don't anticipate stopping any time soon! Block continues to be a work of heart and we enjoy creating every single issue just for you.

Along with publishing Block, the business also continued to grow. As it grew, so did our need for places to put fabric! That's how our town became the home of a dozen unique quilt shops. Twelve years ago, we had just one little brick quilt shop, but then we started selling many different types of fabric and we thought it would be a good idea to group them by style. The individual quilt shops then came about naturally. The main street in town had many empty storefronts and we have purchased them and fixed them up one by one to house each different fabric

collection. All our lives, we never had the money for a brand new house, but we had plenty of fixer uppers. My kids took on each new project with enthusiasm because they weren't afraid of these old buildings. And look at what they've become!

Over the past decade, our hometown has been revitalized. Gone are the empty storefronts and crumbling streets. Now, strolling down the main street in Hamilton is a joy as I walk past thoughtfully restored quilt shops filled with beautiful fabrics, bursting with inspiration for quilters of all kinds, along with a Sewing Center for retreats, a Community Theater, an Education Center, and so much more. In just a few short years, Missouri Star grew from a tiny family business to include an entire community! It was not what I originally had in mind. It's so much better.

JENNY'S FAVORITE

DISAPPEARING PINWHEEL ARROW

There are endless ways to arrange the Disappearing Pinwheel block and this is just one of the many settings, but it's definitely unexpected.

One of my favorite things in quilting, and in life, is seeing the unexpected. Life is full of surprises and if we have the right attitude, they can become opportunities instead of obstacles. I have the same perspective with quilting and while a nice reliable pattern is great, I love seeing "what happens if."

When I'm experimenting with new quilt blocks, you'll often find me in my studio, winging it with a stack of precuts and a prayer, and I'm always amazed at what happens! I like to begin with a traditional quilt block like a four-patch, a nine-patch, an hourglass block, or in this case, a pinwheel. Then I make a few strategic cuts, rearrange the pieces, and sew them back together to make an entirely new block. These "disappearing" blocks have quickly become my favorites!

In this special Best of Block issue, I've chosen the Disappearing Pinwheel

Arrow quilt *(see page 76 for the pattern)* as my favorite for a reason. When I cut up a pinwheel to see what would happen, I never expected to find an arrow. There are endless ways to arrange the Disappearing Pinwheel block and this is just one of the many settings, but it's definitely unexpected. It seems to tell me that there are many paths in life and many ways to do things right. It reminds me of J.R.R. Tolkien who famously wrote, "Not all who wander are lost." Sometimes when life's path takes an unexpected turn, you find out that it wasn't a wrong turn after all. The Cheshire Cat in *Alice and Wonderland* also said, "Well, some go this way, and some go that way. But as for me, myself, personally, I prefer the short-cut." I completely agree! This block might look like it took ages, but we know the real secret!

Creating a Quilt:
FROM TO-DO TO TA-DA!

Making a quilt from start to finish is a wonderful creative journey. I like to savor each step, from measuring and cutting to quilting and binding. There are learning opportunities throughout and while it can be a challenge for a first-time quilter to see how it all comes together, I assure you, it's entirely doable. Here are a few tips to help you on your way as you stitch up your beautiful quilted creation. I can't wait to see what you make! Share your projects with us at **#msqcshowandtell** on social media.

Cutting Fabric

To get started, gather up your rotary cutter, ruler, and cutting mat. Remember your rotary cutter has a razor-sharp blade, so be careful and protect your fingers. Every time you're done cutting, make sure you close it up! And when the blade gets dull, change it right away so you can keep cutting smoothly.

Before you cut any fabric with a rotary cutter, put your cutting mat down to protect the table. It has a handy grid on it to help you line up your fabric as you cut. The ruler will help you as you cut your fabric. Line up your ruler with the grid on the cutting mat. Then, when you cut, you'll get a nice, straight line. Always cut away from yourself and keep your fingers far away from the blade using smooth, steady pressure.

Sewing

Once you have your fabrics cut, it's a good idea to change out your needle before you begin sewing. Use an 80/12 size universal quilting needle. It's good for medium weight fabrics like quilting cotton. Also make sure you're using quality thread; 50wt cotton thread is great for piecing. Be sure to change your needle after about 8 hours of sewing.

If your machine has a foot with a ¼" seam guide, attach it to your machine to help you keep a consistent seam allowance. If you don't have one, use a piece of tape or a seam guide to stay on track, but don't be obsessed with perfection. It's more important to have a consistent seam allowance than a perfect ¼" seam. It will all work out in the end.

Pressing Seams

As you sew blocks together, take care to keep your seams at a consistent ¼". Trim your blocks before you sew them together into rows. As you press your seam, when possible, press to the dark side. That way your darker seams will not show through lighter fabrics. As you create your rows of blocks, pay attention to which direction you are pressing the seams so that your seams will nest. Press one row of blocks one direction

Start Off on the Right Foot

If your machine has a foot with a ¼" seam guide, attach it to your machine to help you keep a consistent seam allowance. If you don't have one, use a piece of tape or a seam guide to stay on track.

and then press the next row the opposite direction. As you sew the rows together, match up the seams, pin them, and then you'll find that they nest together neatly, creating less bulk.

When you're finished sewing your entire quilt top together, trim the entire top with a large ruler and your rotary cutter to square up the sides and get it ready for basting. Give your quilt top a good pressing with some starch or flattening spray. It's so much easier to work with a quilt top that isn't wonky and seams that lay nice and flat.

Backing

Once you've pieced your beautiful quilt top, it's time to choose your backing! Using 108″ wide backing does make things easier, but if you are using standard 42″ wide fabric, you may need to piece your fabric together to cover the entire back of your quilt.

Measure the length and width of your quilt top. Add an extra 8 inches to both the length and width of your quilt if it's going to be machine quilted. Trim off all selvages and use a ½″ seam allowance when piecing the backing. Sew the pieces together along the longest edge. Press the seam allowance open to decrease bulk. Use horizontal seams for smaller quilts (under 60″ wide) and vertical seams for larger quilts. It's a good

idea to choose a backing layout that best suits your quilt. Think about the direction of the pattern and pattern matching. If the print is directional, try to orient it so it makes sense with the front of your quilt.

As for quilting thread color, white, gray, or beige thread blends well with just about anything. If you have a darker backing, you may choose to match your bobbin thread with the backing and keep your top thread a lighter color so it blends well. If you're feeling bold, use a contrasting color of thread that stands out. It's all up to you!

Binding

The last step in creating your quilt is binding. Call me crazy, but I savor this part. I could easily stitch my binding on with a machine, but I love hand tacking my binding while I watch one of my favorite shows on the couch. It's just so cozy. You can create your own binding or you can buy it, but I often make binding from a jelly roll as it's already 2½″ and ready to go.

To make your binding, cut fabric straight across from edge to edge or width of the fabric. You can cut it on a 45° angle into 2½″ strips to create bias binding, which is recommended for curved or scalloped quilt edges. Sew your binding strips together with diagonal seams using the plus sign method. Press your joined binding strips in half and you're ready to sew your binding onto your quilt.

Press to the Dark Side

As you press your seams, when possible, press to the dark side. That way your darker seams will not show through underneath lighter fabrics.

How to join two binding strips together: Lay one strip across the other with the right sides together, like a plus sign. Stitch from the top inside to the bottom outside corners crossing the intersections of fabric as you sew. Trim the seam down to ¼″ and press that center seam open to reduce bulk. Join as many strips together as you need to equal the perimeter of the quilt (the sum of all the edges) plus about 15″ to 20″ inches more to finish.

When you go to sew your binding onto your quilt top, it's a good idea to sew your binding onto the front side of your quilt with your sewing machine, that way it looks nice and neat, and then hand stitch your binding onto the back side of your quilt with an invisible slip stitch (see page 25). Always sew your binding onto your quilt with a ¼″ seam allowance, leaving a 10″ tail of binding at the beginning and the end. It helps to pin or clip the binding to the quilt at the two points where the binding starts and stops. This takes the pressure off of the binding tails while you work. Start sewing your binding on in the middle of a longer side. When you get to a corner, here's how you get those nice mitered corners.

Plus Sign Method

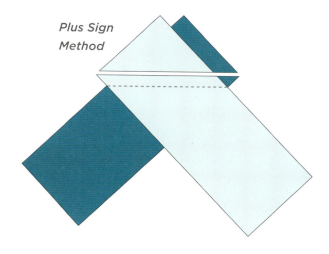

STEP 1

Begin sewing your binding onto the front side of your quilt top, beginning in the middle of a longer side. Use a ¼″ seam allowance.

STEP 2

Stop sewing about ¼″ from the corner and take a little backstitch. Mark this point to help see where to stop your needle.

STEP 3

Pull your quilt out from under the presser foot and clip your threads.

Mitered Corners

Stop sewing about ¼″ from the corner and take a little backstitch. Pull your quilt out from under the presser foot and clip your threads. Flip the binding up at a 90° angle to the edge just sewn. It will form a little triangle with the tail of the binding pointing straight up. Then, fold your binding back down from the top edge, right next to the side that will be sewn next, aligning the raw edges. Then you'll sew from the top fold down on the next side, doing a little backstitch right at the beginning. Later on when you open up the corner, you'll find the most perfect little mitered corner right there!

On Pins and Needles?

Do you ever poke yourself when finishing up your binding? Avoid the ouchies and use amazing Wonder Clips instead of pins to hold your binding in place while stitching. They're especially helpful with keeping corners nice and neat. You'll need about 50 for a lap quilt.

STEP 4

Flip the binding up at a 90° angle to the edge just sewn. It will form a little triangle with the tail.

STEP 5

Fold your binding back down from the top edge, right next to the side that will be sewn next, aligning the raw edges. Continue sewing along the edge until you reach the next corner and repeat.

STEP 6

Stop sewing when you have 12″ left to reach the start of where you began attaching your binding. Lay the binding tails over each other and see where they overlap. At the point where they meet, press a crease into the binding strips, folding back the excess. At that fold, measure 2½″ inches of overlap and trim off the rest of the binding strip.

Closing Binding

Stop sewing when you have 12″ left to reach the start of where you began attaching your binding. You should have two 10″ tails of binding at the beginning and at the end. Lay the binding tails over each other and see where they overlap. At the point where they meet, press a crease into the binding strips, folding back the excess. At that fold, measure 2½″ of overlap and trim off the rest of the binding strip.

To join those two strips, use the plus sign method again, except this time when you're making the plus sign, match the edges. Using a pencil or washable pen, mark your sewing line because you won't be able to see where the corners intersect. Then, sew across from the top inside corner to the bottom outside corner again. Press your seam open, then press the entire binding section in half again and it should lay neatly against the edge of your quilt. You can now stitch it down entirely. When your binding is attached to the front of your quilt, flip the edge over and then stitch it down onto the back side of your quilt. And that's it, friends! You made your very own quilt! I knew you could do it.

STEP 7

Join two strips, using the plus sign method again, except this time when making the plus sign, match the edges. Using a pencil or washable pen, mark your sewing line. Stitch along this line. Trim ¼" from stitch line and press your seam open. Press the entire binding section in half again and it should lay neatly against the edge of your quilt.

Finishing your very own quilt can be a pleasure; it's just as satisfying as licking the spoon when you're all through frosting a cake. Taking the time to enjoy each step makes it even better. Instead of rushing through, treat it as an exercise in patience and find joy in your journey to the finished product. I often speak of quick and easy, and while that's true for many patterns, quilting is still a creative process to be enjoyed. It really does make a difference to thoughtfully finish a quilt with skill. It takes your project to the next level and helps your quilt last longer as the years go by. I hope these tips help you create even more beautiful quilts that will be treasured for a lifetime. Now, let's get stitching!

STEP 8

You can now stitch the edge down entirely. When your binding is attached to the front of your quilt, flip the edge over and then stitch it down onto the back side of your quilt.

Give it the Slip

A slip stitch or ladder stitch is a great way to sew binding on. To begin, tie a knot in the end of your thread and pull it through the edge on the back side of your binding. Fold your binding over and put your needle back in right there, being careful not to go through the front of the quilt. Stitch to the left, through the middle layer about a ¼" or so and poke your needle back up through the backing and the binding. Right where your thread comes out of the quilt, put your needle back down in and stitch to the left again, repeating the process. Your long stitches should be hidden inside the quilt and only a tiny bit of thread should be visible.

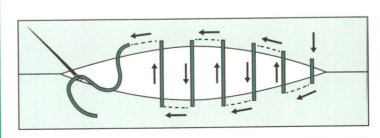

Slip Stitch

USING PRECUTS

Here at Missouri Star Quilt Company, we're all about making quilting and sewing easier and more accessible than ever before and precuts are the best thing since sliced bread! Precut fabrics are packages of fabric that are cut to size in advance. There's no need to cut fabrics for hours; they help you get right to the good part without all the fuss. Almost every single Missouri Star pattern is made to be used with precut fabrics so all you need to know is how many precuts to choose of each size and you're good to go!

The Best of Block contains 25 projects handpicked especially for precuts, along with a few tips and tricks to make sewing them together fast and fun. When you begin quilting with precut fabrics, it really couldn't be any easier. Keep on reading and learn how to make the most of each type of featured precut.

10"

10" PRECUT | *LAYER CAKE*

Layer cakes sound so delicious, don't they? These lovely stacks of fabric help big, beautiful quilts come together in a snap! Whenever I get my hands on one, they don't last long. I can't help but cut into them and get right to the good part—sewing! These fantastic 10" squares are perfect for quilters who are just starting out because of their versatility. You can do so much with a simple square. For example, you can make a quick set of eight half-square triangles with just two 10" squares. It's absolutely magical.

5"

5" PRECUT | *CHARM PACK*

Prepare to be charmed! Charm packs are so cute and so easy to use. I like to keep them on hand for quick projects. They're like potato chips, I can't just have one! I've got to get a whole bunch and before you know it, I've quickly used them right up without a single regret. These wonderful stacks of 5" squares can be used as-is for easy patchwork quilts or you cut them up into neat little quilt blocks that couldn't be simpler to create. Some of my favorite 5" square quilts include Falling Charms, anything made with the Half-Hexi Template and sweet little Periwinkle blocks. I've even created a brand new Happy Little Houses quilt block made especially for the Best of Block.

2½"

2½" PRECUT | *JELLY ROLL*

This is how we roll! Jelly rolls or 2½" strips are one of the most popular precuts out there for a reason. They look so cute all rolled up and they are incredibly useful. It's almost a shame to open them up for a project, but it's totally worth it. If you've ever spent a good amount of time trying to cut perfect strips, you know how valuable these rolls are! From log cabin quilts to sashing and binding, 2½" strips get the job done. You can even slice them up into mini charms and use them to snowball corners and add cornerstones. There are just so many uses for these simple strips!

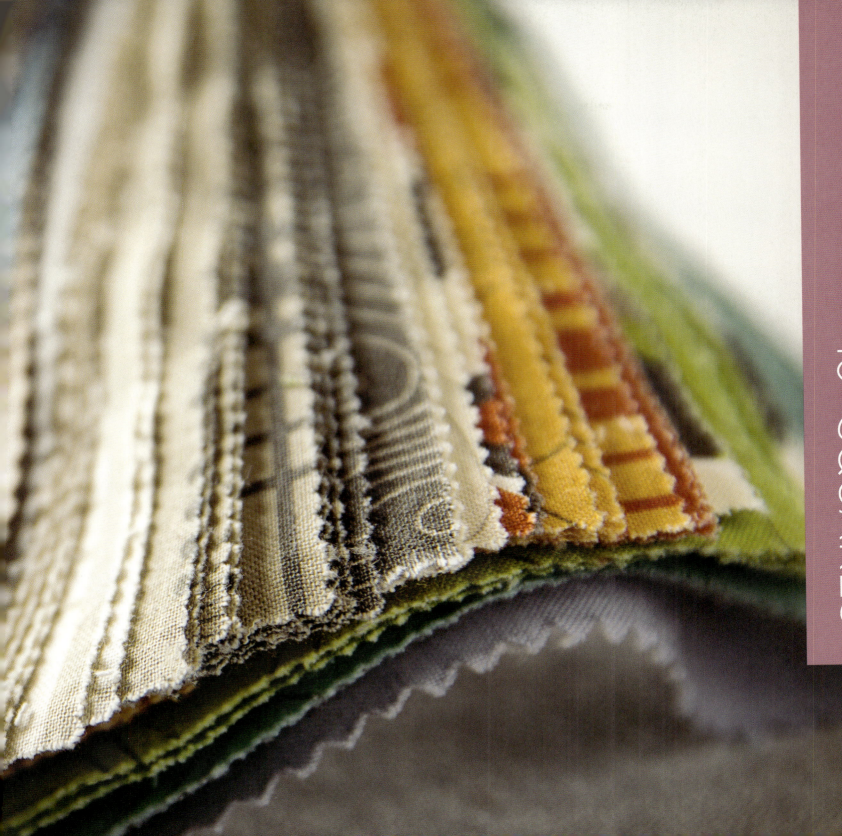

10" SQUARES

PRECUT GUIDE

10" SQUARES | 10" x 10" *typically 42 squares in a package*

How many do I need?
1 = Twin
2 = Queen
2-3 = King

Make your own package of 10" squares
3¼ yards required of various fabrics

How many prints come in a precut package? 16 - 24

Tip for Working with Precuts
Precuts should never be prewashed. If you do, they will distort and fray at the edges, plus your washing machine will be filled with more lint than you can imagine! Just trust me, don't prewash and you're good to go! If you're concerned about bleeding, simply throw a few color catchers in the wash with your finished quilt or wash your quilt with a special detergent called Synthrapol to remove excess dye.

How many ways can you cut up a 10" square?

(2) 5" x 10" rectangles

(4) 5" x 5" squares

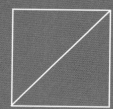
(16) 2½" x 2½" squares

(2) 10" 90° triangles

(4) 10" 90° triangles

(4) 2½" x 10" rectangles

(8) 2½" x 5" rectangles

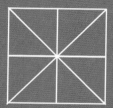
(8) 5" 90° triangles

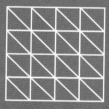
(32) 2½" 90° triangles

10"

SQUARES

These gorgeous quilt patterns have been handpicked especially for 10"
squares. Because this is the biggest precut square, it lends itself well
to larger-scale patterns and also makes a great background square for
appliqué. And remember, one pack of 10" squares is equal to four packs of
5" squares, so they are often interchangeable, depending on the pattern.
Simply pick out your favorite packs of 10" squares, sew along with these
easy-to-follow patterns, and before you know it, you'll have a lovely quilt
to cuddle up with. Keep on reading and learn how to make the most of this
marvelous precut. I have a feeling it'll be a piece of cake!

DISAPPEARING HOURGLASS 2

My mom worked one summer while we were renovating the house. Being twelve, I had been given some new responsibilities to help her out like checking the mail, vacuuming, and putting dinner in the oven. It was kind of exciting, experiencing this newfound maturity. I wanted to show that I could be trusted, so I tried my very best, but sometimes my playful nature got the better of me.

The house had been without a working oven for a few weeks, but finally the new kitchen was put in and it was marvelous. At the time it was absolutely chic, decked out in avocado appliances with shiny chrome trim. I was in awe as I stroked each gleaming surface, imagining myself as a housewife with my very own family, cooking in such a beautiful kitchen.

One fateful day, my mom left me a short note explaining what would be for dinner that night. On the counter next to the note was a large can that read, "English Beef Pie." I skimmed the note and thought, *simple enough*, turned the oven to 400°, peeled the label off the can, placed it in a baking tin, and set it inside the oven. I dusted my hands off, feeling accomplished, and went into the living room to kick back and watch a little TV. But I had made a critical error.

As the can baked in the oven, the pressure built up inside and it exploded like a bomb! From the living room, I heard something that sounded like a gunshot coming from the kitchen. I jumped off the sofa and rolled onto the floor, worried that I was under attack. Hearing nothing else, I crept into the kitchen to find absolute carnage. The beautiful new oven door had been blown off and the remains of the English Beef Pie was spattered all over the spotless linoleum floor and sparkling formica countertops. I was dumbfounded. How had this happened?

As I stood amidst the wreckage, unsure of what do to, my mom suddenly walked into the kitchen and gasped. My dad just shook his head, suppressing a laugh, as my mom slowly picked up a sponge and started cleaning it all up. I snapped out of my shock and started wiping the floor. Later on, they kindly reminded me to read all of the instructions on the can and to open it up next time. I wasn't in trouble, but I had definitely learned my lesson! Thankfully, I don't think another can of English Beef Pie ever showed up in our house ever again.

MATERIALS

QUILT SIZE
79" x 90"

BLOCK SIZE
11½" unfinished, 11" finished

QUILT TOP
1 package 10" print squares
1 package 10" background squares

INNER BORDER
¾ yard

OUTER BORDER
1¼ yards

BINDING
¾ yard

BACKING
8¼ yards - vertical seam(s)
    or 2¾ yards 108" wide

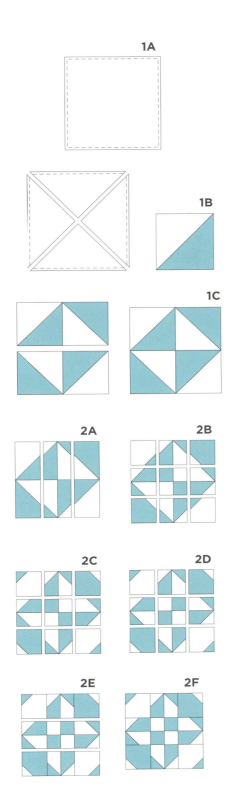

1 hourglass units

Pair a print square with a background square, right sides together. Sew a ¼" seam around the perimeter of the paired squares. **1A**

Cut the sewn squares from corner to corner twice on the diagonal to make 4 half-square triangle units. Open, press, and trim each to 6½". **1B**

Arrange the 4 half-square triangles as shown. Sew the units together in 2 rows and press the seams in opposite directions. Nest the seams and sew the rows together to make the hourglass unit. **Make 42. 1C**

2 block construction

Hint: A rotating cutting mat comes in handy for this section.

Lay an hourglass unit on your cutting surface. Measure and cut 2⅛" from both sides of the vertical center seam. **2A**

Without disturbing the fabric, measure and cut 2⅛" from both sides of the horizontal center seam creating 9 smaller units. **2B**

Turn each of the 4 corner units 180°. **2C**

Turn the center unit 90°. **2D**

Sew the block together in 3 rows as shown. Press the seam allowances of the top and bottom rows toward the left and the seam allowances of the center row toward the right. Nest the seams and sew

the rows together. Press toward 1 side to complete the block. **Make 42. 2E 2F**

Block Size: 11½" unfinished, 11" finished

3 arrange & sew

Refer to the diagram on page 37 as necessary to lay out your units in **7 rows** of **6 blocks.** Notice the blocks are turned 90°. Sew the blocks together in rows. Press the seam allowances of all odd-numbered rows to the left and all even-numbered rows to the right. Nest the seams and sew the rows together. Press to complete the center of the quilt.

4 inner border

Cut (8) 2½" strips across the width of the inner border fabric. Sew the strips together end-to-end to make 1 long strip. Trim the inner borders from this strip.

Measure, cut, and attach the inner borders. The strips are approximately 77½" for the sides and approximately 70½" for the top and bottom.

5 outer border

Cut (8) 5" strips across the width of the outer border fabric. Sew the strips together end-to-end to make 1 long strip. Trim the outer borders from this strip.

Measure, cut, and attach the outer borders. The strips are approximately 81½" for the sides and approximately 79½" for the top and bottom.

6 quilt & bind

See pages 18-25 for tips on finishing your quilt!

1 Pair a 10″ print and background square, sew a ¼″ seam around the edges. Cut the sewn squares twice on the diagonal to make 4 half-square triangles.

2 Arrange the 4 half-square triangles as shown. Sew rows together first; then attach the top to the bottom—just like a 4-patch.

3 Measure 2⅛″ to cut each side of the center seam. The (9) individual blocks should measure 4¼″ square. Be careful not to move the block as you make your cuts.

4 Turn each of the corner squares 180°; the center square 90°. Sew the block together in 3 rows.

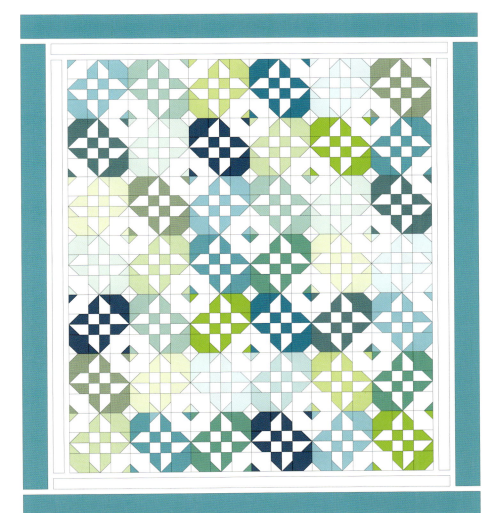

BLOCK
FUN FACT

BABIES FOR DAYS

"I have so many moments that I've loved over the years, but one of my favorite moments was when we were shooting for the baby issue of Block and all the babies were laying in a row on my floor. I had the job of trying to stand out of shot but to get them all to look up at the camera. So I climbed up on my kitchen island and just smiled and waved at all their sweet faces while the photo team got photos from the balcony. It was so ridiculous and fun! I also really love that we've not only been able to have beautiful photos of our families documented through this journey, but the rest of our employee family as well. If you go back to the early issues, there are so many kids and members of our company that you can see grow through the years."

—Misty Doan

Get Ahead of the Curve

Supplies Needed:
Cutting Mat
Rotary Cutter (28mm for curves)
Quarter Inch Foot/Seam Guide
Spray Starch (not flattening spray)
Iron
Missouri Star Drunkard's Path
   Circle Template Set
Thin Pins (that don't bend)
50wt Thread
Your Favorite Fabrics!

Optional:
Rotating Cutting Mat
Wool Pressing Mat

Have you conquered curved piecing yet? If you can sew a ¼" seam, you can sew curves. Seriously! With a few pins, plenty of patience, and a ¼" seam allowance you can piece beautiful curves without shedding a single tear! Quilting really takes on new life when you move beyond the boundaries of straight lines to lovely curved shapes. It gives your quilts a gorgeous, organic quality that feels more human. After all, we are made up entirely of curves! Our body bends and stretches to allow greater movement and using non-linear shapes opens up quilt designs to limitless possibilities.

We'll start with a few easy tips and tricks for sewing the traditional Drunkard's Path block. Once you've got that basic shape down, there's so much you can do! It all begins with fabric preparation, using templates properly, precise cutting, pinning, and learning how to match fabric up when piecing. Curves aren't dangerous anymore, it'll be smooth sailing from here on out.

Fabric Preparation

Fabric naturally has a tendency to stretch, especially on the bias, and when you are sewing curves you are inevitably working with fabric that has been cut on the bias. To achieve better results with curved piecing, preparation is key! There are many pressing sprays out there, but spray starch is the way to go when you're piecing curves. You can find it at the grocery store and it doesn't cost a pretty penny. We like to use Faultless Premium Starch, but any brand will do. It washes out when you're finished sewing and gives fabric much-needed structure to avoid distortion or fraying and give you a crisp, clean result.

To apply spray starch, preheat your fabric with a hot, dry iron. Don't use steam or it will add moisture to your fabric and take the starch out. Once your fabric is preheated, spray it with an even, thin coat of starch, and set it with the iron. When your fabric is dry on one side, flip it over and do the same thing on the opposite side.

You may be wondering, should fabrics be prewashed before curved piecing? In most cases, we do not recommend prewashing fabric unless it has a tendency to bleed. Fabric fresh off the bolt will work great for curved piecing once it is starched.

Curved Templates

Here at Missouri Star we have a few nice options for curved piecing: the Drunkard's Path template in both large and small sizes, the Orange Peel template in large, small, and mini, and the Apple Core template in large and small. Using acrylic templates makes cutting accurate curved pieces easy!

Cutting Curves

When you go to cut your fabrics, be sure to use a cutting mat as usual, place your template securely, and cut along the straight edges first. Then, angle yourself well so that you can cut around the curve without cutting toward yourself. If you happen to have a rotating cutting mat it would definitely come in handy here. As you cut, be sure that you're holding your rotary cutter blade perpendicular

No Slip Solution

If your plastic template tends to shift a little when you're cutting, give it some traction by using the Missouri Star Template Handle, the Gypsy Gripper, some Invisigrip on the bottom side of the template, adhesive sandpaper dots, or even a few pieces of flexible, clear medical tape.

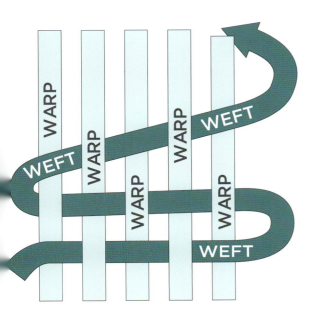

Make the Cut

Before you begin cutting, it's important to change out your rotary blade if it's dull because making more than one pass on a curve can be tricky. Start with a sharp blade so you can slice with confidence!

to the fabric and not at an angle for more accurate results.

Warp & Weft

A note about stretch in fabric. When you are cutting fabric, it is important to pay attention to the warp and weft of the fabric weave. Warp refers to the vertical threads in the weave and weft refers to the horizontal threads in the weave. Fabric will not stretch as much vertically as it does horizontally, so keep this in mind. Just take out a piece of quilting cotton and test it out. Pull it vertically, along the selvage and you'll notice it doesn't budge much. But, when you pull it horizontally, perpendicular to the selvage, it does stretch a bit. When you cut your starched fabrics, do your best to cut the pieces so that the warp and weft go in the same direction. That way, as you piece your fabrics together, they will not stretch in opposite directions and will come together more smoothly.

Pinning Curves

Before you start pinning, fold each of your two Drunkard's Path pieces in half, aligning the corners, and finger press them to find the halfway points on the outer (convex) curves and the inner (concave) curves. Once you have found those points, add pins right there in the center to keep your place. Do the same thing with the point halfway between the middle and each corner to find the quarter-way point and place pins there as well.

Here's where it gets interesting. Go ahead and flip your concave piece over so that the middle point is aligned with the middle point on the convex piece with right sides together. It looks like it won't fit correctly at all because they are curved opposite of each other, but have no fear. With some clever pin placement, they'll go together like magic! Pin the two pieces of fabric together at the center point and then go to your quarter-way points and pin those pieces of fabric together as well. Finally, go to the corners and really do your best to make sure they are aligned and pin them together. Feel free to add extra pins in between each of the pins you've already placed, being sure to align the edges of the fabric. The top piece of fabric will look ruffled for now, but once you sew it down, it will look wonderful after you press it!

Thinner pins that don't bend easily work better when piecing curves because they don't have as much wiggle room. Thicker pins can leave a margin of error, so be sure to grab a fresh set of pins.

Piecing Curved Blocks

If you haven't yet, now is the time to change out your sewing machine foot to that handy ¼" foot. If you don't happen to have one of those (it might be time to get one!) grab some painter's tape and mark the ¼" seam on your sewing machine's stitch plate

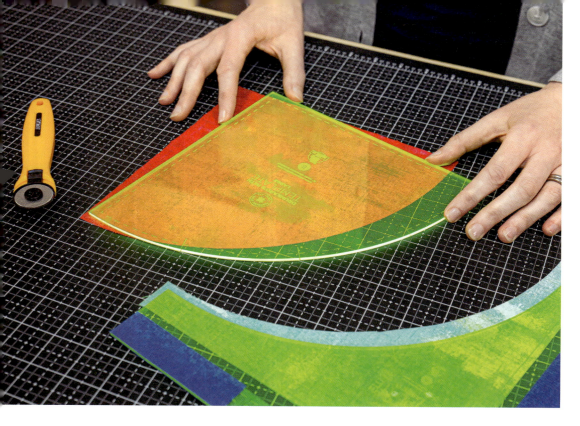

All's Wool That Ends Wool

A wool pressing mat makes your seams lay even flatter and is a great tool to have when quilting. It insulates and radiates heat through both sides of the fabric much better than typical ironing boards. And don't be too sheepish about the scent. It's just a little ewe-nique.

so you can keep your seam nice and consistent. When you start sewing, go slow, pull pins out before you get to them, and most importantly, relax. Keep your shoulders from getting tight, take a few deep breaths, and go for it!

Start with your needle in the down position in your fabric and take a couple backstitches to begin. Follow the curve around nice and steady, smoothing the wavy parts of the curve down as you go and making sure you don't have any creases. If you happen to feel a crease, stop your machine, pull the nearest pin out, make a few adjustments to the fabric so it lays flat again, realign the raw edges and keep

going. Backstitch at the end once more and you're through. Remember, you're the boss of the fabric so show it who's in charge!

Pressing Curved Blocks

When you're finished sewing your curved pieces together, your block will still look a little ruffled, but that's what your iron is for! Be sure to keep the steam off so there's no moisture. You'll want to keep the starch in your block. Press and don't iron back and forth. As you go along the curved seam, press the top of the block down toward the convex part of the block in the middle. It's a good idea to press from the middle toward the edges. Once you've pressed your

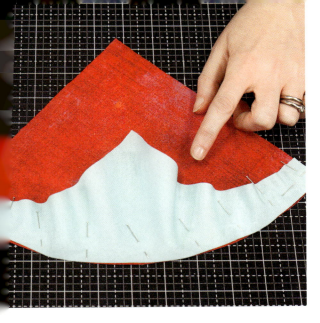

block from the back, turn it over and press again from the front. That's it! You've got a perfectly pressed, curved quilt block. You did it!

For even more awesome curved quilting tips (and a totally free quilt pattern!) check out Sheri Cifaldi-Morrill's online quilting class "Piecing Curves with Confidence" in our Missouri Star Academy class offerings.

The Long and Short of it

Set your stitch length to be slightly shorter at 2mm than you might typically use when piecing (2.5-3mm) because it helps as you round those gentle curves. If your machine has the option to set a slower speed, go ahead and slow down your pace just for now as well. Remember, slow and steady wins the race!

DRUNKARD'S DOTS

You'll go dotty for this updated Drunkard's Path quilt design. It makes use of both the Large and Small Missouri Star Drunkard's Path templates for double the fun! When these cute dots combine, they form a retro-tastic pattern that looks like a cute bow tie or a piece of hard candy. To begin, pick out your favorite packages of 10" print squares along with a package of 10" background squares. You'll also need ½ yard each for an inner and middle border as well as 1¼ yards for the outer border. Connect the dots and see what you can create!

MATERIALS

QUILT SIZE
73" x 73"

BLOCK SIZE
10" unfinished, 9½" finished

QUILT TOP
1 package of 10" print squares
1 package of 10" background squares

INNER BORDER
½ yard

MIDDLE BORDER
½ yard

OUTER BORDER
1¼ yards

BINDING
¾ yard

BACKING
4½ yards – vertical seam(s)
   or 2¼ yards of 108" wide

ADDITIONAL SUPPLIES
Missouri Star Drunkard's Path Circle
   Template Set - Large
Missouri Star Drunkard's Path Circle
   Template Set - Small

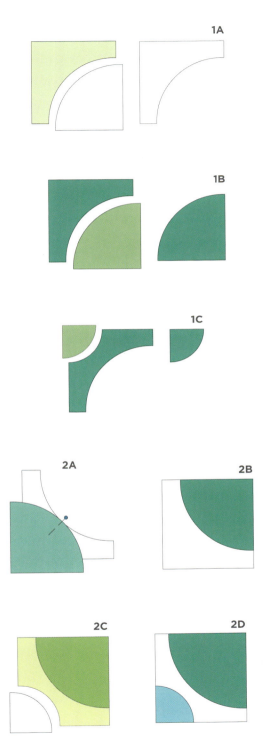

1A

1B

1C

2A

2B

2C

2D

1 sort & cut

Set 6 of the lightest prints from your package of 10″ print squares and 6 background squares aside for another project.

Place 1 background square on your cutting surface. Lay the large template A on top of your square aligning the 3 corners. Carefully cut around the curve. Repeat to cut a **total of 36** background large A pieces. **1A**

Note: The smaller quarter-circle will be cut from the background in a later step.

Place a 10″ print square on your cutting surface. Lay the large template B on top of your square, aligning the 2 sides. Carefully cut around the curve and set the large B piece aside for the moment. **1B**

Lay the small template B on the opposite corner of your print square, again aligning the 2 sides, and cut the small B piece and set aside for the moment. Repeat to cut a **total of 36** large B pieces and a **total of 36** small B pieces. **1C**

2 sew

Pair a large background A piece with a large print B piece. Fold each piece in half on the diagonal and finger press to mark the midway point of each curved edge. Place the large B piece on top of the A piece with right sides facing and finger pressed centers aligned. Pin at the midway point and at both ends of the seam allowance. **2A**

Stitch the 2 pieces together along the curve. Use your fingers to ease in the

fullness around the curve and avoid stretching the fabric as you sew. Press the seam allowance towards the A piece. **Make 36. 2B**

Lay a large Drunkard's Path unit on your cutting surface. Lay the small template A on your unit, aligning the 2 sides of the template with the corner opposite of the sewn quarter-circle. Carefully cut around the curve. Repeat for all remaining Drunkard's Path units. **2C**

Lay out the units in **6 rows of 6** as shown in the diagram on page 49. Pair each unit with a small B piece of a different print. The prints of the small B pieces which meet in the corners should be the same. Repeat the previous instructions to sew the small print B piece to the unit. Press toward the A piece to complete the block. After completing each block, place it back into your quilt top arrangement. Repeat until you have added all 36 B pieces. **2D**

Block Size: 10″ unfinished, 9½″ finished

After you have sewn each block, sew them together in rows. Press the seam allowances of all odd-numbered rows to the left and all even-numbered rows to the right. Nest the seams and sew the rows together. Press toward the bottom.

3 inner border

Cut (6) 2½″ strips across the width of the inner border fabric. Sew the strips together end-to-end to make 1 long strip. Trim the inner borders from this strip.

1 Place 1 background square on your cutting surface. Lay the large template A on top of your square aligning all 3 corners. Carefully cut around the curve. Repeat to cut a total of 36 background large A pieces.

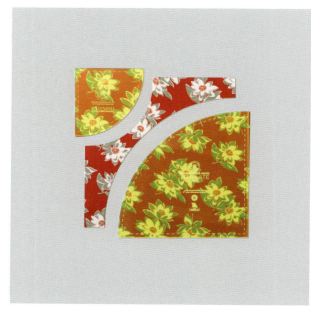

2 Place a 10" print square on your cutting surface. Lay the large template B on top of your square, aligning the 2 sides. Carefully cut around the curve and set the large B piece aside for the moment. Lay the small template B on the opposite corner of your print square, again aligning the 2 sides, and cut the small B piece and set aside for the moment. Repeat to cut a total of 36 large B pieces and a total of 36 small B pieces.

3 Pair a large background A piece with a large print B piece. Fold each piece in half on the diagonal and finger press to mark the midway point of each curved edge. Place the large B piece on top of the A piece with right sides facing and finger pressed centers aligned. Pin at the midway point and at both ends of the seam allowance.

4 Stitch the 2 pieces together along the curve. Use your fingers to ease in the fullness around the curve and avoid stretching the fabric as you sew. Press the seam allowance towards the A piece. Make 36.

48

5 Lay a large Drunkard's Path unit on your cutting surface. Lay the small template A on your unit, aligning the 2 sides of the template with the corner opposite of the sewn quarter-circle. Carefully cut around the curve. Repeat for all remaining drunkard's path units.

6 Repeat the previous instructions to sew the small print B piece to the unit. Press toward the A piece to complete the block. After completing each block, place it back into your quilt top arrangement. Make 36.

Measure, cut, and attach the inner borders. The strips are approximately 57½" for the sides and approximately 61½" for the top and bottom.

4 middle border

Cut (7) 1½" strips across the width of the middle border fabric. Sew the strips together end-to-end to make 1 long strip. Trim the middle borders from this strip.

Measure, cut, and attach the middle borders. The strips are approximately 61½" for the sides and approximately 63½" for the top and bottom.

5 outer border

Cut (7) 5½" strips across the width of the outer border fabric. Sew the strips together end-to-end to make 1 long strip. Trim the outer borders from this strip.

Measure, cut, and attach the outer borders. The strips are approximately 63½" for the sides and approximately 73½" for the top and bottom.

6 quilt & bind

See pages 18-25 for tips on finishing your quilt!

GRAND ADVENTURES

Too often, treasured quilts only see the tops of our beds or the back of the linen closet. Liberate them and take them on outings to your favorite picnic spot or cabin in the woods! This lovely pattern has a tribal aesthetic and seems especially suited to adventures! Wouldn't it look great billowing in the wind on a mountaintop? Begin your quilting quest with two packages of 10" squares, one in a print and one solid. Add a couple yards of complimentary fabric to create borders, stitch it up, and set out with your new quilt tucked under your arm, ready to see the world!

MATERIALS

QUILT SIZE
90¾" x 87¾"

BLOCK SIZE
15½" x 18½" unfinished,
15" x 18" finished

QUILT TOP
1 package of 10" print squares
1 package of 10" background squares

INNER BORDER
¾ yard

OUTER BORDER
1¾ yards

BINDING
1 yard

BACKING
8 yards - vertical seam(s)
   or 2¾ yards 108" wide

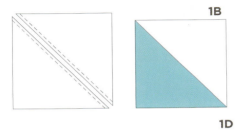

1A

1 make half-square triangles

Mark a line from corner to corner once on the diagonal on the reverse side of 40 background squares. **1A**

Layer the marked square atop a print square with right sides facing. Sew on either side of the drawn line using a ¼" seam allowance. Cut on the drawn line. Open each half-square triangle and press the seam allowance toward the darker fabric. Square the block to 9½". **Make 80**. **1B**

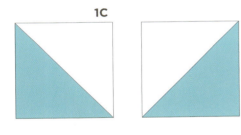

1B

1D

1C

Stack 40 half-square triangles with the center seam going from lower right to upper left. **1C**

Stack the remaining half-square triangles so the center seam is going from lower left to upper right. **1D**

2 block construction

Cut each half-square triangle into (4) 2⅜" strips. **2A**

Swap the placement of the 2 outer strips with each other, then swap the placement of the 2 inner strips with each other. **2B**

Sew the strips together to make 1 quadrant of the block. **2C**

Sew 4 quadrants of differing prints together to complete the block. **Make 20. 2D**

Block Size: 15½" x 18½" unfinished, 16" x 18" finished

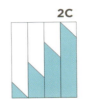

2C

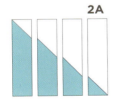

2A

2D

3 arrange & sew

Refer to the diagram on page 55 to lay out your blocks in **4 rows** of **5 blocks** each. Sew the blocks together in rows. Press the seams of all odd-numbered rows to the left and all even-numbered rows to the right. Nest the seams and sew the rows together. Press toward the bottom to complete the quilt center.

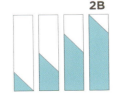

2B

4A

4B

4 inner border

From the 2 remaining 10" print squares, **cut (16)** 2⅜" squares. Fold or mark each square from corner to corner once on the diagonal.

1 Make half-square triangles and stack 40 with the center seam going from lower right to upper left.

2 Stack the remaining half-square triangles so the center seam is going from lower left to upper right.

3 Cut each half-square triangle into (4) 2⅜" strips.

4 Trade the placement of the outer strips of each half-square triangle. Then swap the placement of the 2 inner strips of each half-square triangle.

5 Sew the strips of each half-square triangle together to make 1 quadrant of the block. 2 quadrants are shown above.

6 Sew 4 quadrants together to complete the block.

From the background fabric, cut (8) 2⅜" strips across the width of the fabric. Subcut 1 strip into (4) 2⅜" x 9½" rectangles. Subcut each of 3 strips into (2) 2⅜" x 18½" rectangles for a **total of 6**. Set the remaining strips aside for the top and bottom borders.

Place a print 2⅜" square atop a 2⅜" x 9½" rectangle with right sides facing. Sew on the marked line, then trim the excess fabric ¼" away from the sewn seam. **Make 2** snowballed rectangles with the marked line oriented from bottom right to upper left and **make 2** snowballed rectangles with the diagonal line oriented from bottom left to upper right as shown. **4A**

Place differing 2⅜" squares atop either end of a 2⅜" x 18½" rectangle with right sides facing. Sew on the marked line, then trim the excess fabric ¼" from the sewn seams. Repeat to snowball both ends of the remaining 2⅜" x 18½" rectangles. **4B**

Join (3) 2⅜" x 18½" snowballed rectangles together, then add a 2⅜" x 9½" snowballed rectangle to either end of the strip. Make sure the snowballed end of the shorter rectangle is next to the snowballed end of the longer rectangle. **Make 2** pieced borders.

Sew the remaining 2⅜" strips together end-to-end to make 1 long strip. Trim the inner top and bottom borders from this strip.

Measure, cut, and attach the borders. The pieced borders are approximately 72½" for the sides and the strips are approximately 79¼" for the top and bottom.

5 outer border

Cut (9) 6½" strips across the width of the fabric. Sew the strips together end-to-end to make 1 long strip. Trim the borders from this strip.

Measure, cut, and attach the outer borders. The strips are approximately 79¼" for the top and bottom, and approximately 88¼" for the sides.

Note: The top and bottom outer borders are sewn on first, followed by the side outer borders.

6 quilt & bind

See pages pages 18-25 for tips on finishing your quilt!

55

JUMP RINGS

Go ahead and jump right into this pretty quilt pattern. It's not nearly as difficult as it seems. In fact, it's downright simple. Jump Rings will brighten up your home in an instant and it's sure to make you smile! These elongated oval blocks are created without a single curved seam; it's just amazing how snowballing corners can transform a block. To begin, gather up one roll of your favorite 2½" strips along with 2½ yards of background fabric and 1½ yards of border fabric. Sew it all together and you'll say, "Oh!" when you see these beautiful quilted rings all in a row.

MATERIALS

QUILT SIZE
66" x 81½"

BLOCK SIZE
9" x 10" unfinished,
8½" x 9½" finished

QUILT TOP
1 package 10" print squares
2¼ yards background fabric
 - includes inner border

OUTER BORDER
1¼ yards

BINDING
¾ yard

BACKING
5 yards - vertical seam(s)
 or 2½ yards 108" wide

2A

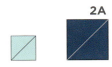

2B   **2C**

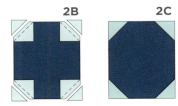

2D

2E

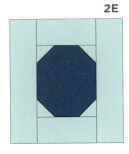

2F

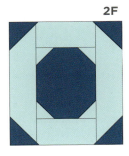

1 cut

From each 10″ square, cut:

- (3) 2½″ strips across the width of the square. Subcut 1 of the strips in half to yield (2) 2½″ x 5″ rectangles.

- (1) 1½″ strip along the width of the remainder of the square. Subcut (4) 1½″ squares from the strip.

Keep all the matching print pieces of each 10″ square together.

From the background fabric, cut:

- (7) 5″ strips across the width of the fabric. Subcut each strip into (6) 5″ x 6″ background rectangles for a **total of 42**.

- (11) 2½″ strips across the width of the fabric. Subcut the strips into 2½″ squares. Each strip will yield up to 16 squares and a **total of 168** are needed.

Set the remaining fabric aside for the inner border.

2 block construction

Select 1 set of matching print pieces, (1) 5″ x 6″ background rectangle and (4) 2½″ background squares. Mark a line from corner to corner on the diagonal on the reverse side of each 1½″ print square and each 2½″ background square. **2A**

Place a marked print square on each corner of the 5″ x 6″ background rectangle with right sides facing, as shown. Sew on the marked lines. Trim the excess fabric away ¼″ away from sewn

seams. Press towards the corners. **Make 42** centers. **2B 2C**

Attach a 2½″ x 5″ matching print rectangle to the top and bottom of the center, as shown. Press towards the print. **2D**

Add a 2½″ x 10″ matching print rectangle to either side of the unit. **2E**

As done previously, lay the marked 2½″ background squares on each corner of the unit. Repeat to sew, trim, and press towards the corners to complete the block. Trim to 9″ x 10″ if needed. **2F**

Block Size: 9″ x 10″ unfinished, 8½″ x 9½″ finished

3 arrange & sew

Refer to the diagram on page 61 as necessary to lay out your blocks in **7 rows** of **6 blocks**. Sew the blocks together in rows. Press the seam allowances of all odd-numbered rows to the left and all even-numbered rows to the right. Nest the seams and sew the rows together. Press to complete the center of the quilt.

4 inner border

Cut (7) 2½″ strips across the width of the background fabric. Sew the strips together end-to-end to make 1 long strip Trim the border from this strip.

Measure, cut, and attach the inner borders. The strips are approximately 67″ for the sides and approximately 55½″ for the top and bottom.

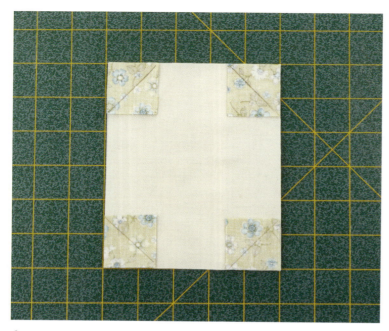

1 Snowball the 5″ x 6″ background rectangle with (4) 1½″ squares of the same print.

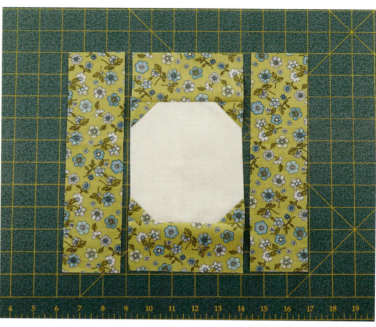

2 Add a 2½″ x 5″ rectangle to the top and bottom and press. Add a 2½″ x 10″ rectangle to both sides and press.

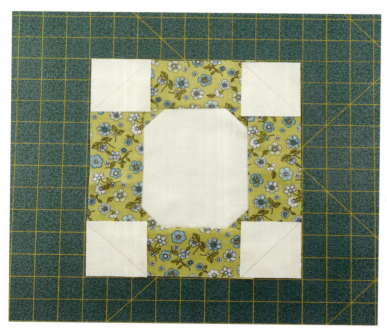

3 Snowball the corners of the block using (4) 2½″ background squares.

4 Trim the excess fabric ¼″ away from the sewn seam.

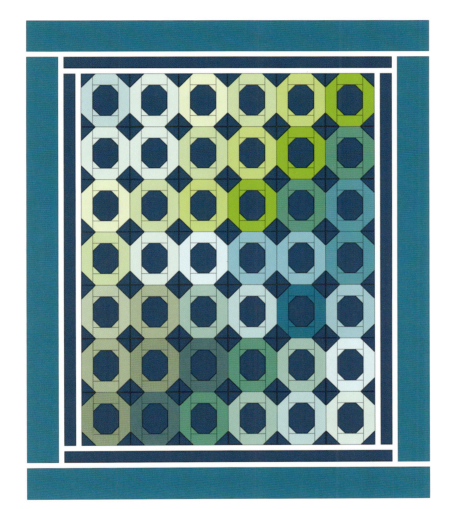

5 outer border

Cut (7) 6″ strips across the width of the outer border fabric. Sew the strips together end-to-end to make 1 long strip. Trim the border from this strip.

Measure, cut, and attach the borders. The strips are approximately 71″ for the sides and approximately 66½″ for the top and bottom.

6 quilt & bind

See pages 18-25 for tips on finishing your quilt!

TOTALLY TULIPS

Tulips aren't just for spring! Enjoy a gorgeous floral display all year long with the Totally Tulips pattern. Each individual flower is pieced from four charm squares and they look so bright and cheery all together. Although it may seem complex, the tulips are constructed from easy snowballed corner units and half-square triangles with a strip for the stem. Simple, right? Start sewing with one package of 10" squares in your favorite prints along with 3¾ yards of background fabric. And guess what? There aren't any weeds to worry about!

MATERIALS

QUILT SIZE
89" x 90"

BLOCK SIZE
9½" x 17½" unfinished,
9" x 17" finished

QUILT TOP
1 package 10" print squares
¼ yard solid - tulip stems
3¾ yards background fabric
   - includes inner border

OUTER BORDER
1½ yards

BINDING
¾ yard

BACKING
7 yards - vertical seam(s)
   or 2¾ yards of 108" wide

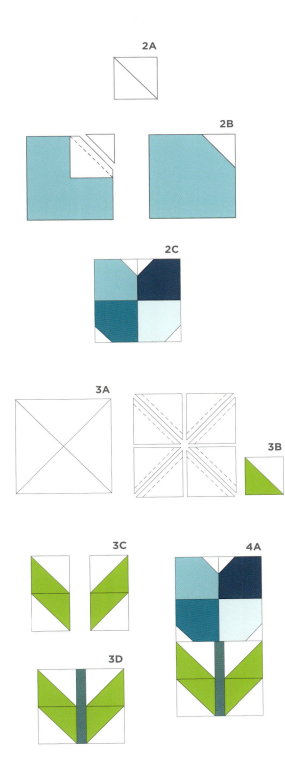

2A

2B

2C

3A

3B

3C

3D

4A

1 cut

Select (28) 10" print squares. Cut each in half vertically and horizontally to make 5" squares for a **total of 112.** The remaining squares will be used for "leaves".

From the ¼ yard of solid fabric, cut:

- (1) 8½" strip across the width of the fabric. Subcut a **total of (28)** 8½" x 1½" rectangles.

From the background fabric, cut:

- (4) 10" strips across the width of the fabric. Subcut the strips into 10" squares. Each strip will yield 4 squares and a **total of 14** are needed. Set the extra squares aside for another project.

- (14) 2½" strips across the width of the fabric. Subcut 7 strips into 2½" squares. Each strip will yield 16 squares and a **total of 112** squares are needed. Subcut the remaining 7 strips into 2½" x 9½" rectangles. Each strip will yield 4 rectangles and a **total of 28** are needed. Set these pieces aside to use for sashing rectangles.

- Set the remaining fabric aside for the long sashing strips and the inner border.

2 blossom units

On the reverse side of the 2½" squares, mark a line from corner to corner once on the diagonal either by folding the square and pressing a crease or by marking it with a pencil. **2A**

Place a marked background square atop a 5" print square with right sides facing. Sew

on the marked line. Trim the excess fabric away ¼" from the sewn seam. Press toward the snowballed corner. **Make 112. 2B**

Arrange 4 snowballed squares together in a 4-patch formation as shown. Sew the units together in 2 rows and press in opposite directions. Sew the rows together. Press 1 direction. **Make 28** tulip blossom units and set aside for the moment. **2C**

3 leaf units

On the reverse side of (14) 10" background squares, draw a line from corner to corner twice on the diagonal. **3A**

Layer a marked square with a 10" print square, right sides facing. Sew on either side of both drawn lines using a ¼" seam allowance. Cut the sewn squares through the center horizontally and vertically, then cut on the drawn lines. Open each section to reveal a half-square triangle. Each set of sewn squares will yield 8 half-square triangles and a **total of 112** are needed. Square each half-square triangle unit to 4½" and stack the matching half-square triangles together. **3B**

Pick up 4 matching half-square triangles. Sew 2 together in a vertical row as shown. Notice the direction in which the half-square triangles are placed. Sew the other 2 matching half-square triangles together in the same manner. Notice the half-square triangles are placed in the opposite direction of the first row, creating a mirror image. Press. **3C**

1 Place a marked background square atop a 5″ print square with right sides facing. Sew on the marked line, then trim ¼″ away from the sewn seam.

2 Press the seam allowance of the snowballed square toward the print fabric. Make 4.

3 Sew 4 snowballed 5″ squares together in a 4-patch formation as shown to create a blossom unit.

4 Make leaf units by stitching 2 half-square triangles together vertically. Notice the 2 leaf units are mirror images of each other. Sew a leaf unit to either side of a 1½″ x 8½″ solid rectangle.

5 Sew a blossom unit top to a leaf unit to complete the block.

6 Add a 2½″ x 9½″ background rectangle to the bottom of 14 tulip blocks. Sew a 2½″ x 9½″ rectangle to the top of the remaining blocks.

5A

Sew the vertical rows to either side of a 1½" x 8½" solid rectangle. Press. **Make 28** leaf units. **3D**

4 block construction

Sew a blossom unit to a leaf unit as shown and press to complete the block. **Make 28** blocks. **4A**

Block Size: 9½" x 17½" unfinished, 9" x 17" finished

5 horizontal sashing

Sew a 2½" x 9½" background rectangle to the bottom of 14 blocks. Sew a 2½" x 9½" background rectangle to the top of the remaining blocks. **5A**

6 arrange & sew

Lay out the blocks in *vertical* rows with each row having **4 blocks**. Begin the first row with blocks that have the background rectangle sewn to the bottom of the block. Alternate that row with blocks that have the background rectangle sewn to the top of the block. Continue on in this manner until you have **7 rows**. Sew the rows together vertically when you are happy with the arrangement.

7 make vertical sashing strips

From the remaining background fabric, cut (12) 2½" strips across the width of the fabric. Remove the selvages and sew 2 strips together end-to-end. Measure the

row of blocks and trim the strip to your measurement. It should be approximately 76½". **Make 6**.

Join the vertical rows, adding a sashing strip between each to complete the center of the quilt top.

8 inner border

Cut (8) 2½" strips across the width of the fabric. Sew the strips together end-to-end to make 1 long strip. Trim the inner borders from this strip.

Measure, cut, and attach the inner borders. The strips are approximately 76½" for the sides and approximately 79½" for the top and bottom.

9 outer border

Cut (9) 5½" strips across the width of the fabric. Sew the strips together end-to-end to make 1 long strip. Trim the outer borders from this strip.

Measure, cut, and attach the inner borders. The strips are approximately 80½" for the sides and approximately 89½" for the top and bottom.

10 quilt & bind

See pages 18-25 for tips on finishing your quilt!

IRISH CHANGE

Is it time for a change? This pretty pattern is very similar to the beloved Irish Chain, except there's a little more going on in the background! It's the perfect pattern to show off your favorite beautiful prints in between the chain blocks. You'll be astounded at how simple it truly is. Each of the traditional Irish Chain blocks is created with quick strip piecing and the other blocks are uncut 10" squares. That's it! Begin sewing with a package of 10" squares, 1½ yards of the right accent fabric, and 3¼ yards of background fabric to bring it all together. You'll really change things up with this quilt.

MATERIALS

QUILT SIZE
100½" x 100½"

BLOCK SIZE
10" unfinished, 9½" finished

QUILT TOP
1 package 10" print squares
1½ yards accent fabric
3¼ yards background fabric
   - includes inner border

OUTER BORDER
1¾ yards

BINDING
1 yard

BACKING
9¼ yards - vertical seam(s)
   or 3¼ yards 108" wide

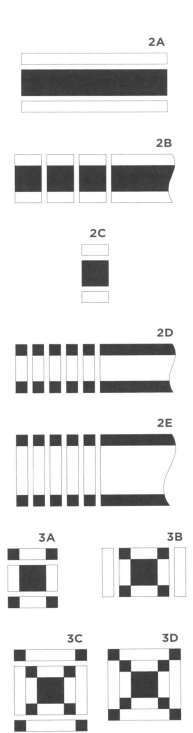

1 cut

From the accent fabric, cut:
- (16) 2" strips across the width of the fabric.

- (5) 4" strips across the width of the fabric. From 1 strip, subcut (1) 4" square and set the remainder of the strip aside for another project.

From the background fabric, cut:
- (8) 2" strips across the width of the fabric.

- (4) 4" strips across the width of the fabric. Subcut (1) 4" x 2" rectangle from each of 2 strips.

- (8) 7" strips across the width of the fabric. Subcut 4 strips into 7" x 2" rectangles. A **total of (82)** 7" x 2" background rectangles are needed.

2 make units

A units

Using a ¼" seam allowance, sew a 2" background strip to the top and bottom of a 4" accent strip. Press the seams toward the center. **Make 4. 2A**

Cut each of these strip sets into (10) 4" increments to create A units. **2B**

Sew a 4" x 2" background rectangle to the top and bottom of the 4" accent square to create 1 additional A unit for a **total of 41.** Press the seams towards the accent fabric. **2C**

B units

Sew a 2" accent strip to the top and bottom of a 4" background strip. Press the seams toward the accent fabric. **Make 4.**

Cut each of these strip sets into (21) 2" increments to create a **total of 82** B units. **2D**

C units

Sew a 2" accent strip to the top and bottom of a 7" background strip. Press the seams toward the background fabric. **Make 4.**

Cut each of these strip sets into (21) 2" increments to create a **total of 82** C units. **2E**

3 block construction

Lay 1 A unit and 2 B units in 3 rows as shown. Nest the seams and sew the rows together to complete the block center. Press. **3A**

Sew a 7" x 2" background rectangle to either side of the block center. Press the seams toward the outside edges. **3B**

Sew a C unit to the top and bottom of the center unit, nesting the seams as you go. Repeat the instructions above to **make 41** blocks. Press. **3C 3D**

Block Size: 10" unfinished 9½" finished

4 arrange & sew

Refer to the diagram on page 73 to lay out your blocks and 10" print squares in **9 rows** of **9 blocks,** alternating your pieced blocks with print squares. Each

1 Sew a 2" background strip to the top and bottom of a 4" accent strip. Press the seams toward the center. Make 4. Cut each of these strip sets into (10) 4" increments to create A units.

2 Sew a 2" accent strip to the top and bottom of a 4" background strip. Press the seams toward the accent fabric. Make 4. Cut each of these strip sets into (21) 2" increments to create a total of 82 B units.

3 Sew a 2" accent strip to the top and bottom of a 7" background strip. Press the seams toward the background fabric. Make 4. Cut each of these strip sets into (21) 2" increments to create a total of 82 C units.

4 Lay 1 A unit and 2 B units in 3 rows as shown. Nest the seams and sew the rows together to complete the block center.

5 Sew a 7" x 2" background rectangle to either side of the block center. Press the seams toward the outside edges.

6 Sew a C unit to the top and bottom of the center unit, nesting the seams as you go. Repeat the previous instructions above to make 41 blocks. Press.

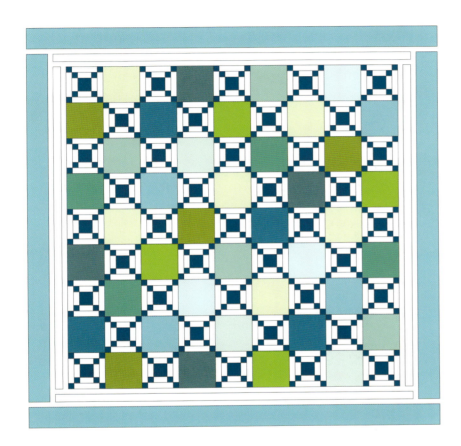

odd-numbered row will begin with a pieced block, and each even-numbered row will begin with a print square. Sew the blocks together in rows. Press the seam allowances of all odd-numbered rows to the left and all even-numbered rows to the right. Nest the seams and sew the rows together to complete the quilt center.

5 inner border

Cut (9) 2½" strips across the width of the fabric. Sew the strips together end-to-end to make 1 long strip. Trim the inner borders from this strip.

Measure, cut, and attach the inner borders. The strips are approximately 86" for the sides and approximately 90" for the top and bottom.

6 outer border

Cut (10) 6" strips across the width of the fabric. Sew the strips together end-to-end to make 1 long strip. Trim the outer borders from this strip.

Measure, cut, and attach the outer borders. The strips are approximately 90" for the sides and approximately 101" for the top and bottom.

7 quilt & bind

See pages 18-25 for tips on finishing your quilt!

DISAPPEARING PINWHEEL ARROW

One year my high school offered an alternative to traditional physical education and my reaction was, "Alright, sign me up!" It was archery, and I thought, *How hard can it be? Bow, arrow, target, done!* Imagine my surprise when on my first day of class, I found myself with a bow in one hand and the string for it in the other. We started from square one learning how to string our own bows. Then we moved on to detailed instruction about fletching arrows, the effect of feathers, the basic physics of a straight shot, and what felt like an unabridged history of archery from the dawn of time.

Then came the moment, my moment to finally shoot the bow! I had learned how to string it so carefully and when I held it in my hands, it felt powerful. Remember how I thought archery would be "Bow, arrow, target, done"? Well, that first time it was more like "Bow, arrow, flop." You might think I'd be discouraged, but instead, I was hooked. I love a good challenge! I actually enjoyed practicing and got better and better. There was even one time I shot an arrow with such intensity that the string took some of the skin on my arm with it, but I liked to think it just made me tougher.

Studying archery was very satisfying, but I didn't realize how valuable it was to me until I had my seven kids and they all wanted to learn how to shoot a bow and arrow. We went out into the woods together and searched out just the right wood to make their own bows and arrows. I remember very clearly teaching them that if they wanted their arrows to fly true they needed straight sticks.

As I watched them search for the perfect sticks for their arrows, I couldn't help but think about how lucky I was to be their mother, to be there to watch them learn and grow. There's a Bible verse about children in Psalms 127: 5 that says, "Happy is the man that hath his quiver full of them." And I couldn't have been happier to see my gaggle of little archers running through the woods. It's always exciting to release an arrow and watch where it will fly. The same goes for children. My hope is that I have given them the ability to fly sure and true.

MATERIALS

QUILT SIZE
81" x 92"

BLOCK SIZE
11½" unfinished, 11" finished

QUILT TOP
1 package 10" print squares
1 package 10" background squares

INNER BORDER
¾ yard

OUTER BORDER
1¾ yards

BINDING
¾ yard

BACKING
7½ yards – horizontal seam(s)

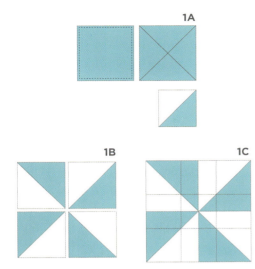

1A

1B   1C

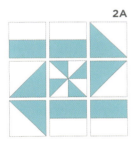

2A

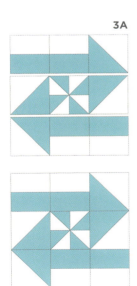

3A

1 make half-square triangles

Layer a 10″ print square with a 10″ background square, right sides facing. Sew all the way around the outside edge using a ¼″ seam allowance. Cut the sewn squares from corner to corner twice on the diagonal. Open and press the seam allowance toward the darker fabric. Each set will yield 4 half-square triangles. You need a **total of 168** half-square triangles or 42 sets. Trim each half-square triangle to 6½″. **1A**

Sew 4 half-square triangles together to make a pinwheel. **1B**

Measure your sewn block. Divide your measurement by 3 so you can cut your block into thirds. It should be about 4⅛″. Divide that number in half if you would like to use the center seam as a guide. If you're using the center seam, measure out 2¹⁄₁₆″ inches (or half of your measurement) and cut on either side of the center seam horizontally and vertically. **1C**

2 trading places

The center pinwheel does not move. Arrange the outer units as shown to create a top arrow pointing to the right and a bottom arrow pointing to the left. Align (2) 2-patch pieces end-to-end to form an arrow shaft in the first and third rows of the block. **2A**

3 block construction

You now have the pieces that make up 3 rows of a 9-patch block. Sew the pieces into rows as shown, then sew the rows together to complete the block. **Make 42** blocks. **3A**

Block Size: 11½″ unfinished, 11″ finished

4 arrange & sew

Arrange the blocks into rows with each row having **6 blocks** across. Notice that every other block is turned, altering the direction the arrows point. **Make 7 rows.** When you are happy with the way the quilt is laid out, sew the blocks together. Press the odd-numbered rows toward the left and the even-numbered rows toward the right.

Nest the seams and sew the rows together. Press the seams in 1 direction to complete the quilt center.

5 inner border

Cut (8) 2½″ strips across the width of the fabric. Sew the strips together end-to-end to make one long strip. Trim the borders from this strip.

Measure, cut, and attach the inner borders. The strips are approximately 77½″ for the sides and approximately 70½″ for the top and bottom.

1 Layer a 10″ print square with a 10″ background square with right sides facing. Sew all the way around the perimeter using a ¼″ seam allowance.

2 Open to reveal 4 half-square triangles. Press. Square each half-square triangle to 6½″.

3 Sew the 4 half-square triangles together to form a pinwheel.

4 Cut on either side of the center seam horizontally and vertically.

5 Rearrange the pieces as shown. Sew the pieces together to form rows. Press the seams in opposite directions.

6 Nest the seams and sew the rows together. Press in 1 direction to complete the block.

6 outer border

Cut (9) 6″ strips across the width of
the fabric. Sew the strips together end-
to-end to make one long strip. Trim
the borders from this strip.

Measure, cut, and attach the outer
borders. The strips are approximately
81½″ for the sides and approximately 81½ ′
for the top and bottom.

7 quilt & bind

See pages 18-25 for tips on finishing
your quilt!

LATTICE ARROWS

Point these arrows in all four directions and your quilt will hit the mark every time! This lovely pattern has an intriguing lattice design that shapes the arrows, making the flying geese that are formed seem to float on air, creating wonderful dimension. It may look like a brain-buster, but it couldn't be simpler. Believe it or not, it's created almost entirely from half-square triangles! To start, you'll need one package of 10" print squares, 4½ yards of complimentary fabric, 2½ yards in a secondary color, and 1¼ yards of background fabric. Aim high and let it fly!

MATERIALS

QUILT SIZE
88" x 88"

BLOCK SIZE
9½" unfinished, 9" finished

QUILT TOP
1 package 10" print squares
4½ yards dark blue fabric
  - includes outer border
2½ yards green fabric
1¼ yards white solid
  - includes inner border

BINDING
¾ yard

BACKING
8 yards – vertical seam(s)
  or 2¾ yards of 108" wide

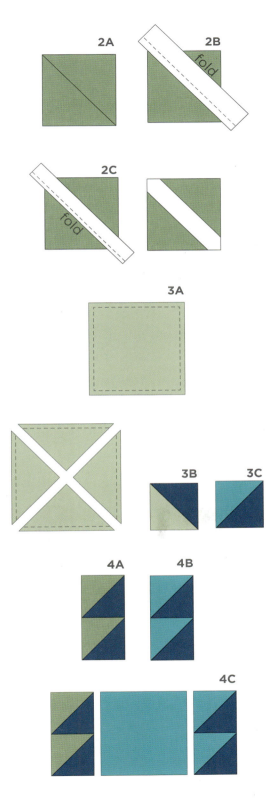

1 sort & cut

Cut each of (32) 10" print squares in half vertically and horizontally and set the remaining squares aside for another project. Each square will yield (4) 5" squares and a **total of (128)** 5" print squares are needed. Keep matching squares together in pairs.

From the dark blue fabric, cut (20) 5" strips across the width of the fabric. Subcut each strip into (8) 5" squares for a **total of (160)** 5" dark blue squares. Set the remaining fabric aside for the outer border.

From the green fabric, cut:
- (12) 5" strips across the width of the fabric. Subcut each strip into (8) 5" squares for a **total of (96)** 5" green squares.
- (9) 2¾" strips across the width of the fabric. Subcut each strip into 2¾" squares. Each strip will yield up to 15 squares and a **total of (128)** 2¾" green squares are needed.

From the white solid fabric, cut (5) 4¼" strips across the width of the fabric. Subcut each strip into 4¼" x 1½" rectangles. Each strip will yield up to 28 rectangles and a **total of (128)** 4¼" x 1½" lattice rectangles are needed. Set the remaining fabric aside for the inner border.

2 make lattice squares

Draw a line corner to corner once on the diagonal on the right side of each 2¾" green square. **2A**

Fold a 4¼" x 1½" lattice rectangle in half lengthwise with wrong sides facing. Align the long raw edges of the lattice rectangle with the marked diagonal on the green square, as shown. Stitch the rectangle to the square using a ¼" seam allowance. **2B**

Fold the rectangle back over the seam and press. Topstitch along the folded edge close to the edge. Trim the edges of the rectangle even with the green square to complete the lattice unit. **Make 128** lattice units and set them aside for the moment. **2C**

3 make half-square triangles

Pair a 5" green square with a 5" dark blue square, right sides facing. Sew around the perimeter using a ¼" seam allowance. **3A**

Cut the sewn square from corner to corner twice on the diagonal to yield 4 half-square triangle units. Open, press, and trim each unit to 2¾". Repeat with the remaining 5" green squares and 95 dark blue squares for a **total of 384** green/dark blue half-square triangles. **3B**

Choose a matching pair of 5" print squares. In the same manner as before, pair a 5" print square with a 5" dark blue square, right sides facing. Repeat the previous instructions to make print/dark blue half-square triangles using 1 print square from each pair. **3C**

Keep the 4 print/dark blue half-square triangles and matching 5" print squares

1 Fold a 4¼" x 1½" lattice rectangle in half lengthwise, wrong sides facing. Align the long raw edges of the lattice rectangle with the marked diagonal on the green square. Stitch the rectangle to the square using a ¼" seam allowance. Fold the rectangle back over the seam and topstitch along the folded edge. Trim the edges of the rectangle even with the square to complete the lattice unit. Make 128.

2 Pair a 5" green square with a 5" dark blue square, right sides facing. Sew around the perimeter using a ¼" seam allowance. Cut the sewn squares from corner to corner twice on the diagonal to yield 4 half-square triangle units. Open, press, and trim each unit to 2¾". Repeat to make a total of 384 green/dark blue half-square triangles.

3 Repeat the previous instructions to make print/dark blue half-square triangles using 1 print square from each pair. Make 64 sets of 4 matching print/dark blue half-square triangles.

4 Sew 2 green/dark blue half-square triangles together as shown. Sew 2 print/dark blue half-square triangles together as shown. Sew the 2 green/dark blue half-square triangles to the left side of the 5" print square. Sew the 2 print/dark blue half-square triangles to the right side of the print square.

5 Arrange 1 lattice unit and 3 green/dark blue half-square triangles as shown. Sew the units together to create the top row. Arrange 1 green/dark bluehalf-square triangle, 2 print/dark blue half-square triangles, and 1 lattice unit as shown. Sew the units together to create the bottom row. Arrange the top, center, and bottom rows as shown.

6 Nest the seams and sew the rows together to complete the block. Press the seams to 1 side. Make 64 blocks.

together. **Make 64** sets of matching print squares and half-square triangles.

4D

4E

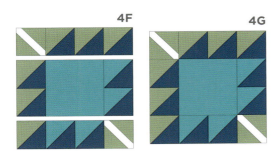

4F

4G

4 block construction

Select 1 set of 1 print square and 4 matching half-square triangles, 2 lattice units, and 6 green/dark blue half-square triangles.

Sew 2 green/dark blue half-square triangles together as shown. Press the seam toward the bottom. **4A**

Sew 2 print/dark blue half-square triangles together as shown. Press the seam toward the top. **4B**

Sew the 2 green/dark blue half-square triangles to the left side of the 5" print square. Sew the 2 print/dark blue half-square triangles to the right side of the print square. Press towards the half-square triangles to create the center row. **4C**

Arrange 1 lattice unit and 3 green/dark blue half-square triangles as shown. Sew the units together and press towards the center to create the top row. **4D**

Arrange 1 green/dark blue half-square triangle, 2 print/dark blue half-square triangles, and 1 lattice unit as shown. Sew the units together and press towards the center to create the bottom row. **4E**

Arrange the top, center, and bottom rows as shown. Nest the seams and sew the rows together to complete the block. Press the seams to 1 side. **Make 64** blocks. **4F 4G**

Block Size: 9½" unfinished, 9" finished

5 arrange & sew

Referring to the diagram below, lay out your blocks in **8 rows** of **8 blocks** each. Pay special attention to the orientation of the blocks. The arrow points of the blocks alternate left and right and the lattice units should meet to form an "X". Sew the blocks together in rows. Press the seam allowances of all odd-numbered rows to the left and all even-numbered rows to the right. Nest the seams and sew the rows together. Press toward the bottom.

6 inner border

Cut (8) 2½" strips across the width of the white solid fabric. Sew the strips together end-to-end to make 1 long strip. Trim the inner borders from this strip.

Measure, cut, and attach the inner borders. The strips are approximately 72½" for the sides and approximately 76½" for the top and bottom.

7 outer border

Cut (9) 6½" strips across the width of the dark blue fabric. Sew the strips together end-to-end to make 1 long strip. Trim the outer borders from this strip.

Measure, cut, and attach the outer borders. The strips are approximately 76½" for the sides and approximately 88½" for the top and bottom.

8 quilt & bind

See pages 18-25 for tips on finishing your quilt!

PRAIRIE FLOWER

A flower in the midst of the wide prairie must have been a very welcome sight indeed. This pleasant Prairie Flower quilt has been adapted from an antique quilt pattern to work with precuts, so it's easy-as-pie. It comes together simply with a few strategically snowballed corners arranged around a center square. Just grab your favorite package of 10″ squares along with 3¼ yards of a solid background fabric and this lovely quilt will be blooming on your bed in no time.

MATERIALS

QUILT SIZE
74" x 89½"

BLOCK SIZE
14" unfinished, 13½" finished

QUILT TOP
1 package 10" squares
3¼ yards background fabric
   - includes sashing and inner border
¼ yard for cornerstones

OUTER BORDER
1½ yards

BINDING
¾ yard

BACKING
5½ yards - vertical seam(s) or
   2¾ yards 108" wide

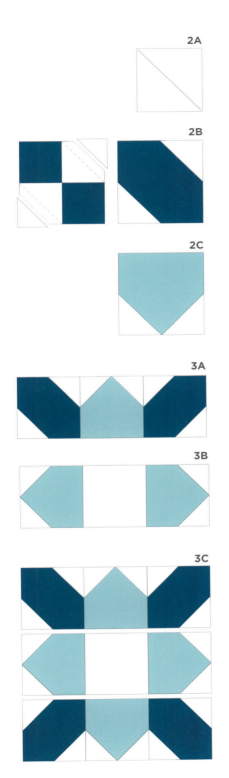

2A

2B

2C

3A

3B

3C

1 cut

From each 10" square, cut:

- (4) 5" squares for a **total of 160** squares.

From the background fabric, cut:

- (20) 2½" strips across the width of fabric. Subcut the strips into 2½" squares for a **total of 320**.

- (3) 5" strips across the width of the fabric. Subcut the strips into 5" squares for a **total of 20.**

- (11) 2½" strips across the width of the fabric. Subcut the strips into (31) 2½" x 14" rectangles for sashing.

From the cornerstone fabric, cut:

- (1) 2½" strip across the width of fabric. Subcut the strip into 2½" squares for a **total of 12**.

2 block construction

Fold a 2½" square from corner to corner on the diagonal and press the crease in place. The crease marks your sewing line. Prepare (16) 2½" squares. **2A**

Sew a 2½" square onto 2 opposing corners of a 5" square. Trim each ¼" away from the seam line. These units go on the corners of the block. **Make 4** and set them aside for the moment. **2B**

Sew (2) 2½" squares to 2 corners of a 5" square as shown. The squares are on adjacent corners. These units go between the corner units. **Make 4. 2C**

3 sew rows

Sew a corner unit to either side of a center unit as shown. **Make 2** rows like this. **3A**

Sew a center unit to either side of a background 5" square. **Make 1** row like this. **3B**

Sew the three rows together to make 1 block. **Make 20** blocks. **3C**

Block Size: 14" unfinished, 13½" finished

4 arrange & sew

Lay out the blocks in rows, with each row containing **4 blocks.** Once you are happy with the appearance, sew the blocks together into rows adding a 2½" x 14" sashing rectangle between each. **Make 5** rows and press toward the sashing rectangles. **4A**

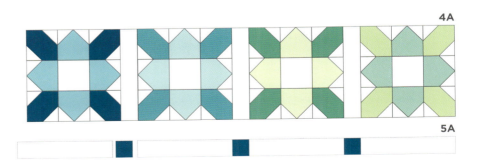

4A

5A

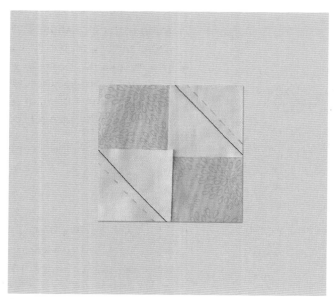

1 Place a 2½" square on 2 opposing corners of a 5" square. Sew along the diagonal of the small squares from corner to corner. Trim the excess fabric ¼" away from the sewn seam.

2 After the unit has been trimmed, open and press.

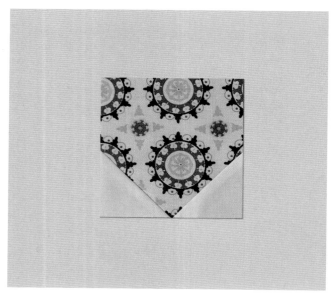

3 Sew a 2½" square on the diagonal of the 2 corners that are adjacent on a 5" print square. Trim the excess fabric away ¼" from the sewn seam allowance, open and press.

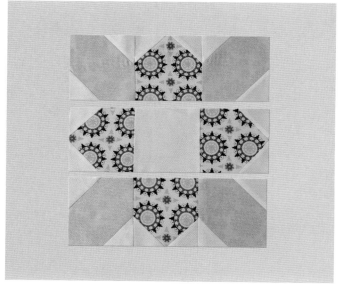

4 Arrange the units into 3 rows as shown and sew the rows together to complete the block.

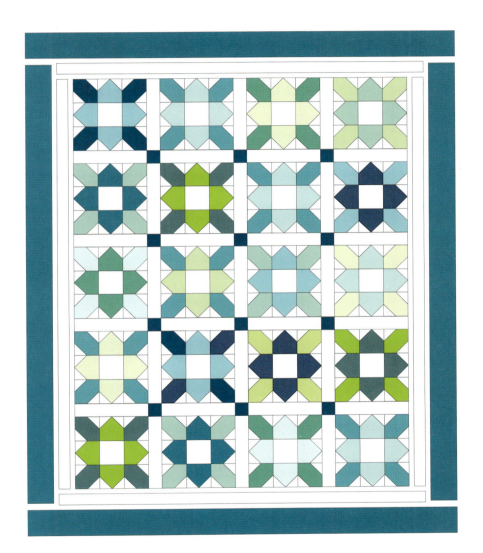

5 sashing strip

Sew a cornerstone square to a 2½" x 14" sashing rectangle. Add a 2½" square, then another sashing rectangle. Continue on in this manner until you have sewn a strip containing 3 cornerstones and 4 sashing rectangles. **Make 4** sashing strips and press towards the sashing rectangles. **5A**

Sew a sashing strip between each row of blocks. Press the seams in 1 direction to complete the quilt center.

6 inner border

Cut (7) 2½" strips across the width of the fabric. Sew the strips together end-to-end to make 1 long strip. Trim the borders from this strip.

Measure, cut, and attach the inner borders. The strips are approximately 76" for the sides and approximately 64½" for the top and bottom.

7 outer border

Cut (8) 5½" strips across the width of the fabric. Sew the strips together end-to-end to make 1 long strip. Trim the borders from this strip.

Measure, cut, and attach the outer borders. The strips are approximately 80" for the sides and approximately 74½" for the top and bottom.

8 quilt & bind

See pages 18-25 for tips on finishing your quilt!

FALL SHENANIGANS

Fall is such a fun time of year. As the leaves turn and the pumpkins and squash start to ripen, I feel the itch to create something special. It's the magical season when I get to embrace my theatrical roots, dust off my costuming skills, and get ready for Halloween!

Halloween is a highly-anticipated event at the Doan house. We take full advantage of the one night each year when we can dress up and get into a few shenanigans without too many questions! Each Halloween we choose a theme, and one year we decided on "The Doan Family Circus."

After a lot of planning, and only a few wardrobe malfunctions, the crew was ready for Halloween night. The house was decorated from top to bottom. I found some red and white striped fabric on the dollar rack and proceeded to turn the front of our Victorian porch into a circus tent! We played circus music and the Doan Family Circus opened for its one night performance.

When all the kids and grandkids started arriving in their clown costumes I just couldn't believe how great everyone looked! Even with dozens of little clowns running around, each one was as different as night and day.

My son-in-law decided to dress as "The Tall Man," a circus sideshow, and I had enough striped material left over from the tent to make him the longest pants in history! He walked on sheet rock stilts and his legs were as long as I was tall. We gave him the job of passing out the candy, and when he bent down with the big bowl of treats, he scared some kids half to death! In some ways my family feels like a circus all year round, but it was great fun to fully embrace our playfulness for just one night.

MATERIALS

WALL HANGING SIZE
40½" x 40"

SUPPLIES
1 package 10" print squares
   (we used Halloween-themed fabric)
½ yard background fabric

BORDER
½ yard

BINDING
½ yard

BACKING
2⅔ yards - vertical seam(s)

OTHER
(1) 4½" x 6½" scrap of Heat n
   Bond Lite
Missouri Star Large Simple Wedge
   Template for 10" Squares

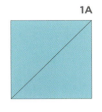

1A

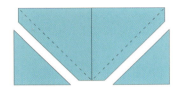

1B

1C

Because there are different elements to make for this quilt, we thought it might be easiest to "cut as we go" when making each section.

Section 1 - Cats

Select (6) 10″ squares, 3 to use as cats and 3 for background.

1 cut

From each of the 3 squares being used for cats, cut: (2) 5″ x 10″ rectangles – trim 1 rectangle to 5″ x 9½″ – subcut the other rectangle into (1) 3″ x 5″ rectangle and (1)2½″ x 5″ rectangle. Cut the 2½″ rectangle into (2) 2½″ squares. Set aside the remaining 4½″ x 5″ rectangle for another project. Keep all matching prints stacked together.

From each of the squares being used as background for the cats, cut: (1) 5″ square, (1) 2½″ x 5″ rectangle, and (1) 2½″ square. Set the remaining fabric aside for another project.

2 sew

Fold 2 matching 2½″ squares from corner to corner once on the diagonal. The fold line marks your sewing line. Place a square on each end of a 2½″ x 5″ background rectangle with right sides facing. Sew along the crease, then trim the excess fabric ¼″ away from the sewn seam. **1A**

Add a matching 3″ x 5″ rectangle to complete the cat's head. **1B**

Sew the cat's head to the left side of a 5″ background square. **1C**

Pick up the matching 5″ x 9½″ print rectangle. Fold a crease from corner to corner once on the diagonal of the 2½″ background square. Place the square on the upper right corner of the print rectangle with right sides facing. Sew along the crease, then trim the excess fabric ¼″ away from the sewn seam. Open and press the seam toward the print fabric. **1D**

Sew the 2 portions together to complete 1 cat block. **Make 3** and sew them together in a horizontal row. **1E**

Block Size: 9½″ unfinished, 9″ finished

1D

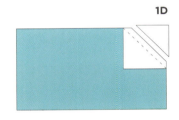

1E

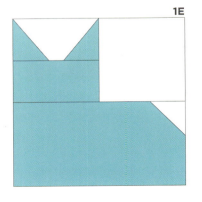

1   Snowball each end of a 2½" x 5" background rectangle using 2½" squares. Sew the snowballed rectangle to a matching 3" x 5" rectangle to make the cat's head. Sew the cat's head to a 5" background square.

2   Using a 2½" square, snowball a matching 5" x 9½" rectangle to make the body of the cat.

3   Sew the top portion of the cat to the body to complete 1 cat.

4   Layer (2) 10" squares with right sides facing. Trim 1" off the bottom and set the strips aside. Center the simple wedge template on the layered pieces and cut through both layers on each side of the template.

5   Sew a background side piece to either side of the center triangle.

6   Stitch the 1" strip that was trimmed off previously to the bottom of the piece to complete the hat block.

Section 2 – Pumpkin

1 cut

From the background fabric, cut a 10" strip and trim to a 10" square. The 27½" rectangles can be cut from the remaining piece of strip.

- Subcut the square in half horizontally and vertically for a **total of (4)** 5" squares.

- (1) 6¼" x 27½" rectangle

- (1) 2¾" x 27½" rectangle

- (1) 2¾" strip across the width of the fabric – subcut the strip into (2) 2¾" x 18½" rectangles.

Select (5) 10" squares. Cut each square in half horizontally and vertically for a **total of (20)** 5" squares.

Trace the pumpkin stem found on page 107 onto the paper side of the fusible. Roughly cut around the stem and press to the reverse side of a contrasting print square. Cut out the stem and set it aside until the pumpkin section is sewn together.

2 sew

Sew (5) 5" squares together into a row. **Make 4** rows. Press the even-numbered rows toward the left and the odd-numbered rows toward the right. Sew the rows together. **2A**

Mark a line, either in pencil or folding and finger pressing a crease, from corner to corner once on the diagonal on the reverse side of each 5" background square. Place a marked square on each outer corner of the sewn rows of squares. Sew on the marked line, then trim ¼" away from the sewn seam. After the corners have been snowballed, open and press the seam allowances toward the pumpkin. **2B**

Sew a 2¾" x 18½" background rectangle to both sides of the pumpkin. Press the seam allowances toward the pumpkin. **2C**

Sew a 2¾" x 27½" background rectangle to the bottom of the pumpkin and a 6¼" x 27½" background rectangle to the top. Press the seams toward the pumpkin. **2D**

Center the pumpkin stem atop the center square in the top row of the pumpkin. Fuse in place, then stitch around the stem using a blanket stitch. **2E**

Block Size: 27½" x 26½" unfinished, 27" x 26" finished

Section 3 – Hats

Select (8) 10" squares—4 light for the background pieces and 4 dark for the prints.

1 cut

Layer a light background square with a dark square with right sides facing. Trim 1" off the bottom of the layered squares. Set the 1" strip aside as that will become the brim of the hat.

2A

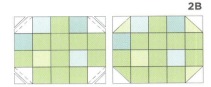

2B

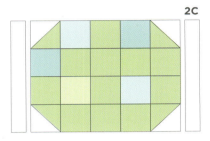

2C

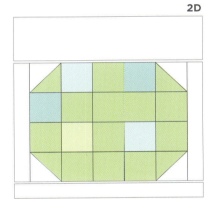

2D

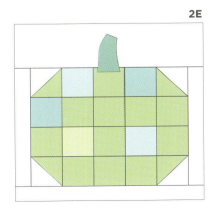

2E

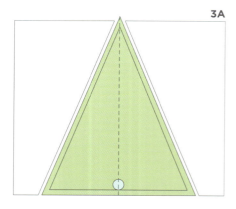

3A

Mark the center of the top layered square along the top edge of the piece with a pencil or by making a crease with your fingernail. Center the simple wedge template on the layered pieces and align the bottom of the template with the bottom on the layered squares. Notice the top of the template extends a little bit above the top edge. Cut through both layers of fabric on each side of the template. **3A**

2 sew

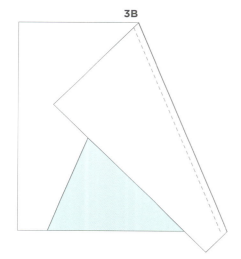

3B

Pick up the background side pieces and sew 1 to either side of the print triangle. Sew the 1″ x 10″ print strip to the bottom and trim to fit. **Make 4** hats. **3B 3C**

Block Size: 9″ x 9¼″ unfinished, 8½″ x 8¾″ finished

Note: You have enough pieces left to make another hat, if you choose to use them. The colors would be reversed, so the hat would be made using the background fabric and the hat backgrounds would be made using prints.

Sew the hats together in a vertical row.

Section 4 - Arrange & Sew

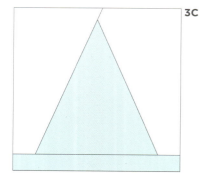

3C

Sew the row of cats to the top of the pumpkin section. Add the row of hats to the right side of the pumpkin/cat section. Refer to the diagram on the next page if necessary.

Section 5 - Borders

Cut (4) 3″ strips across the width of the fabric. Sew the strips together end-to-end to make 1 long strip. Trim the borders from this strip.

Measure, cut, and attach the borders. The strips are approximately 35½″ for the sides and approximately 41″ for the top and bottom.

Section 6 - Quilt & Bind

See pages 18-25 for tips on finishing your quilt!

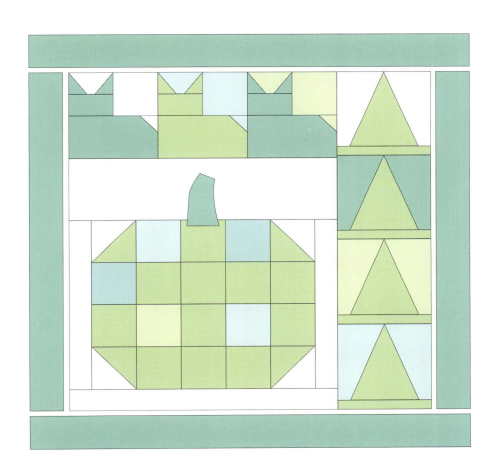

CUTE CAMPER PILLOW

Hit the road with the cutest little camper in tow and you'll be traveling in style wherever you roam! Glamping is the latest craze in road tripping and it's so much fun. Instead of camping out in a cramped tent, travel in style with a souped-up vintage trailer and be sure to adorn it with pretty quilted accents to help you feel right at home. This darling glamper pillow is perfect for making your home away from home even cozier. Start your trip with one pack of 10" print squares, add ½ yard of background fabric, and soon you'll be heading off on your next adventure!

MATERIALS

PROJECT SIZE
Fits a 16" pillow form

BLOCK SIZE
12½" unfinished, 12" finished

PILLOW TOP
1 package 10" print squares
½ yard background fabric

PILLOW BACK
¾ yard

OTHER
(1) ¼" diameter button
(1) ¾" - 1" diameter button
(1) 14" zipper
½ yard Heat n Bond Lite
18" square batting

4A

5A

6A

6B

6C

1 trace

Trace each of the shapes, found on pages 106-107, onto the paper side of the fusible web leaving a little room between the pieces so you are able to cut them apart easily. You will need to trace the camper body, roof, window #1, window #2, both parts of the window #2 curtains, door, tow bar, and tire each once. You will need to trace the flag template 11 times.

Roughly cut the traced pieces apart.

2 sort, fuse, & cut

Sort through your package of 10″ squares and decide which fabrics you'd like to use for each part. Once you've decided, lay a fabric square face down on your pressing surface. Lay the appropriately traced shape of fusible web with the glue side against the wrong side of the fabric. Adhere the fusible web to the fabric following the manufacturer's instructions. Cut the shape out on the traced line and set aside.

Repeat to adhere the traced shapes to the wrong side of the assigned fabric squares. After adhering, cut the shapes out along the traced line and set aside.

3 cut

From the background fabric, cut a 12½″ strip across the width of the fabric. Subcut a 12½″ square and (5) 12½″ x 3½″ rectangles. Subcut each rectangle into (3) 3½″ squares. A **total of (14)** 3½″ squares are needed. Set the 3½″ squares aside to use for the half-square triangles.

4 arrange & fuse

Peel the paper backing off each of your fused shapes. Lay the 12½″ background square right side up on your pressing surface. Arrange the shapes on top of the background square, being sure nothing is within a ¼″ of the outside edge of the block. Shift the shapes around until you're happy with the arrangement. Follow the manufacturer's instructions for your fusible web and adhere the shapes to the background square. **4A**

5 appliqué

Stitch around all of the edges of the fused fabric using a blanket or small zigzag stitch. **5A**

Note: Our flags are fused to the background fabric and sewn with a zigzag stitch around each flag. Along the top is a great place to experiment with decorative stitches, embroidery stitches, or couching to embellish your project. We used a decorative triple stitch along the top of the flags.

Block Size: 12½″ unfinished, 12″ finished

6 sew half-square triangles

Select 14 of the remaining print squares and set the rest aside for another project. From each of the 14 selected squares, cut a 3½″ strip across the width of the square. Subcut a 3½″ square from each strip for a **total of 14**.

Note: You can cut up to (4) 3½" squares from each 10" print square if you wish.

Mark a diagonal line on the reverse side of each of the 3½" background squares. **6A**

Lay a marked background square atop a 3½" print square, right sides facing. Sew on both sides of the marked line using a ¼" seam allowance. Cut on the marked line. Open to reveal 2 half-square triangle units. Press the seam allowances towards the darker fabric and square each unit to 2½". **6B 6C**

Repeat with the remaining 3½" squares to make a total of 28 half-square triangle units.

7 pieced border

Sew 2 matching half-square triangle units together as shown. Press the seam allowances to 1 side. Repeat with all remaining half-square triangle units. **7A**

Sew 3 paired half-square triangle units together and press all seams to 1 side to create a side border. **Make 2** side borders. **7B**

Sew 4 paired half-square triangle units together and press all seams to 1 side to create the top border. Repeat to make a bottom border. **7C**

Sew the side borders to the block. Press the seams towards the block. Sew the top and bottom borders to the top and bottom of the block. Press the seams towards the block. **7D**

8 finish the pillow top

From the pillow backing fabric, cut a 20½" strip across the width of the fabric. Subcut a 20½" square and set the remainder of the strip aside for the pillow back.

Tip: If you'd like to add any embroidery to embellish your pillow top, now is the time!

Layer the pillow top with batting and the 20½" square and quilt. After the quilting is complete, square up the pillow top and trim away all excess batting and backing.

Once your pillow top is quilted and squared, place the 2 buttons on top of the pillow top and stitch in place. The smaller button should go on the camper door to create a doorknob. The larger button should go on top of the tire to create a hubcap. **8A**

9 make the pillow back

From the leftover strip of pillow backing fabric, cut a 20½" x 16½" rectangle. From the 20½" x 16½" rectangle, subcut (2) 8¼" x 16½" rectangles. From the 1" strip that remains, subcut (2) 1" x 3" rectangles.

Place a 1" x 3" rectangle on top of the zipper with right sides facing. Slide the rectangle towards the center of the zipper until it is ½" past the metal stopper. Sew the rectangle to the zipper, backstitching a couple of times to strengthen the seam. **9A**

Trim the zipper just past the raw edge of the rectangle. Fold the rectangle over the

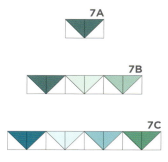

7A

7B

7C

7D

8A

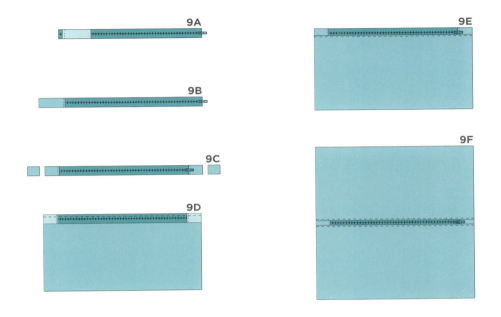

9A

9B

9C

9D

9E

9F

seam and press. Topstitch to finish the zipper tab. **9B**

Repeat to create a zipper tab on the opposite end of the zipper. Find the center of the exposed zipper. Measure 8¼" from the center point and trim the ends. **9C**

Note: You may need to switch the presser foot of your sewing machine to a zipper foot for this part of the project.

Place the zipper face down on top of the bottom portion of the pillow backing. Sew the zipper to the pillow backing. **9D**

Open and press the seam allowance away from the zipper. Topstitch. **9E**

Place the remaining 8¼" x 16½" rectangle on top of the pillow back, right sides facing. Sew the pieces together. Open and press the seam allowance away from the zipper. Topstitch. **9F**

Note: If you switched to zipper foot, this is a good time to switch back to your regular presser foot.

10 finish the pillow cover

Lay the pillow top with the right side facing up. Open the zipper partially and then lay the pillow back on top, right sides facing. Sew around the perimeter of the pillow using a ¼" seam allowance. Finish the edges with a serger or zigzag stitch to prevent fraying.

Clip the corners and turn the pillow right sides out. Insert a pillow form and zip it up closed. Now it's time to enjoy your cute camper pillow!

Cute Camper Template p. 102

Window #1

Cute Camper
Template p. 102

Window #2

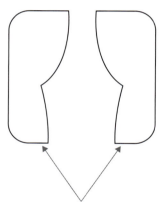

Cute Camper Template p. 102

Window #2

Curtains

Cute Camper Template p. 102

Camper Body

1"

1" Templates included are 100% scale.

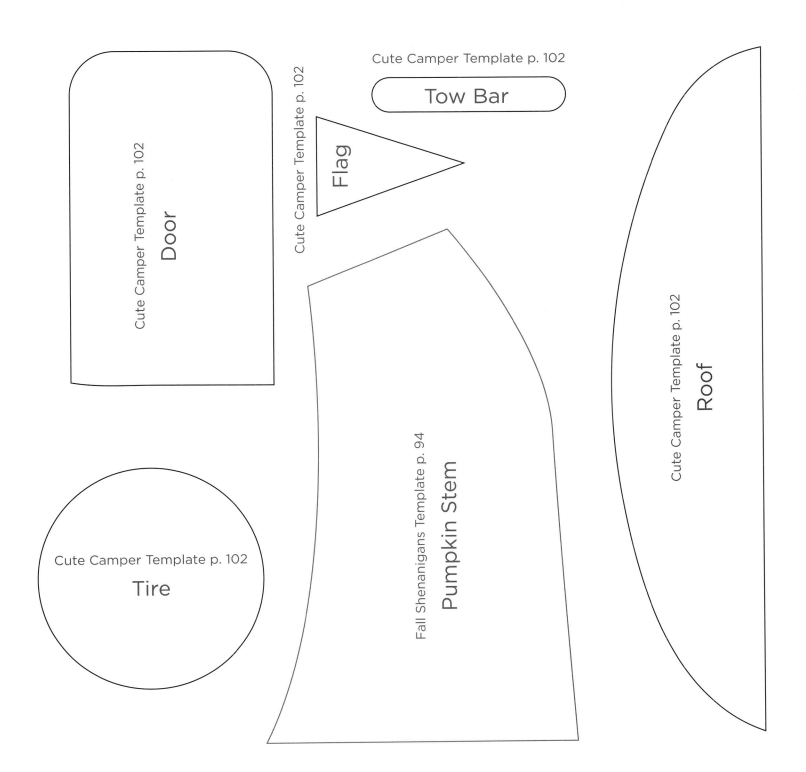

Cute Camper Template p. 102

Door

Cute Camper Template p. 102

Flag

Cute Camper Template p. 102

Tow Bar

Cute Camper Template p. 102

Roof

Cute Camper Template p. 102

Tire

Fall Shenanigans Template p. 94

Pumpkin Stem

Journal

Planning ahead is a quilter's best friend! We've all been in the middle of a project and realized we don't have the fabric we need to get the job done. This handy quilt planner is here to help you keep your ducks in a row. Then, when you're all finished, it's easy to look back on older projects and reminisce.

1 DO YOU START WITH A QUILT DESIGN IN MIND AND THEN FIND THE FABRIC?
OR DO YOU START WITH FABRIC FIRST AND THEN CHOOSE THE DESIGN TO FIT?

2 IF YOU COULD TAKE A CLASS FROM ANY QUILTER, WHO WOULD IT BE?
WHAT WOULD YOU HOPE TO LEARN?

3 DO YOU HAVE A FAVORITE QUILT PATTERN?
WHAT TYPES OF QUILTS ARE YOU ATTRACTED TO?

Quilt Planner

Get inspired for a brand new quilting project with these journal prompts. As you look back on why you began quilting, fresh ideas will come to mind! New techniques, color palettes, and fun patterns are in your future. We're SEW excited to plan ahead with you and help you along on your quilting journey!

PROJECT IDEA _____

_____

_____

FABRICS _____

_____

COLORS

PRECUTS USED _____

_____

_____

YARDAGE _____

BLOCK DESIGN

SIZE _____ **X** _____

SKETCH　　　　　　*SIZE* _____ **X** _____

NOTES _____

_____

_____

_____

_____

_____

_____

_____

Build Your Own

Use this space to sketch or draw your own design based on the patterns in this section.

5" SQUARES

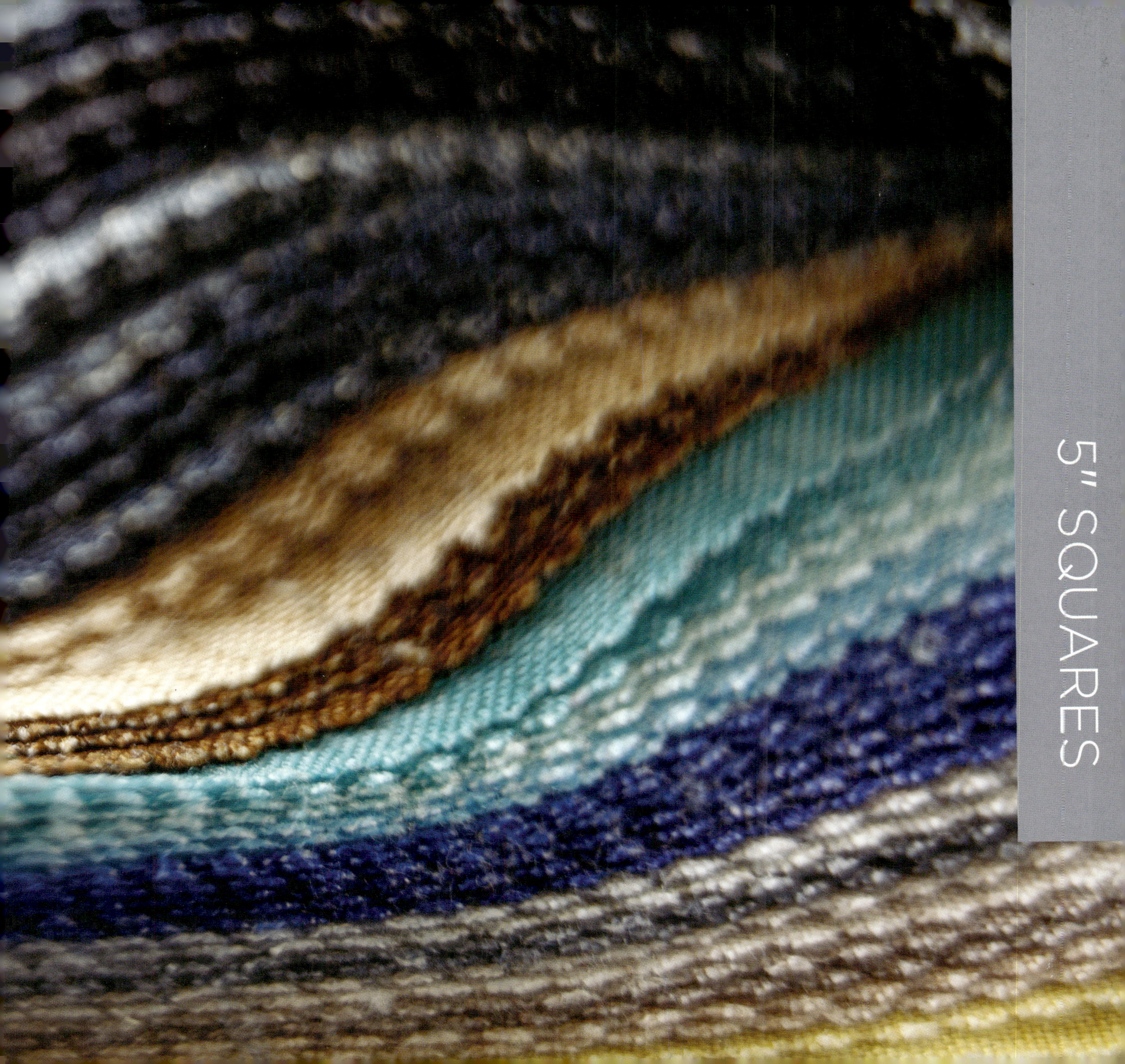

PRECUT GUIDE

5" SQUARES | 5" x 5" *typically 42 squares in a package*

How many do I need?
1=Baby
2=Crib
3=Lap
5=Twin
5-6=Queen
6-7=King

Make your own package of 5" squares
1 yard required of various fabrics

How many prints come in a precut package? 16 - 24

Tip for Working with Precuts
Precuts have pinked edges which keep them from unraveling, but they do shed a lot of lint. If you're concerned about lint control, keep a lint roller on hand to pick up loose threads and fabric trimmings from your sewing table. Don't directly lint roll on your precuts as it may cause them to unravel more easily.

How many ways can you cut up a 5" square?

(2) 2½" x 5" rectangles

(4) 2½" x 2½" squares

(16) 1¼" x 1¼" squares

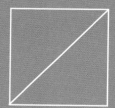

(2) 5" 90° triangles

(4) 5" 90° triangles

(4) 1¼" x 5" rectangles

(8) 1¼" x 2½" rectangles

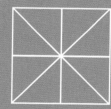

(8) 2½" 90° triangles

5"

SQUARES

In this special issue, I hope you enjoy these darling quilt patterns chosen for 5"
squares, along with handy pointers to make using them easy as pie. Charm pack
patterns are perfect for simple, smaller projects like baby quilts, lap quilts, and
so much more. Go ahead and grab a stack of your favorite 5" squares, stitch
along with these fast, fun patterns, and soon you'll have a quilt that's perfect for
snuggling. Keep on reading and learn how to make the most of this amazing
precut. It's sure to work like a charm!

DIZZY DAISY

Bright daisies whirling and twirling across a quilt is too much fun to miss! You'll love how easily these off-kilter blocks come together. Daisies are truly the friendliest flower and they symbolize innocence, new beginnings, and true love. It's always enjoyable to start a new quilt and you'll fall in love with this easy block! By snowballing three of the corners and arranging each square directionally, the result is a flower with a lot of interesting movement and a diagonal center. It looks like it took ages, but it's a snap! Start with four packages of 5″ squares, add 4¼ yards of background fabric and dig in!

MATERIALS

QUILT SIZE
79" x 90"

BLOCK SIZE
9½" unfinished, 9" finished

QUILT TOP
4 matching packages of
   5" print squares
4¼ yards background fabric
   – includes inner border

OUTER BORDER
1¾ yards - includes cornerstones

BINDING
¾ yard

BACKING
5½ yards - vertical seam(s)
   or 2¾ of 108" wide

2A

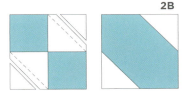

2B

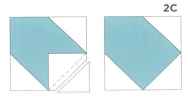

2C

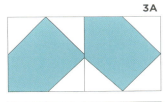

3A

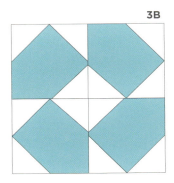

3B

1 cut

From the background fabric, cut (58) 2½" strips across the width of the fabric. Subcut:

- 32 strips into 2½" squares for a **total of 504**.

- 18 strips into 2½" x 9½" rectangles for a **total of 71** rectangles. Set these aside for the sashing.

- Set the remaining strips aside for the inner border.

From the outer border fabric, cut (2) 2½" strips across the width of the fabric. Subcut the strips into 2½" squares. Each strip will yield 16 squares and a **total of 30** squares are needed. Set the squares aside to use as cornerstones in the sashing.

Set the remainder of the fabric aside for the outer border.

2 snowball corners

On the reverse side of each 2½" background square, draw a line or press a crease from corner to corner once on the diagonal. **2A**

Place a marked 2½" background square on 2 opposite corners of a 5" square with right sides facing. Sew on the marked sewing line. Trim the excess fabric away ¼" from the sewn seam and press open. **2B**

Place another 2½" marked background square on 1 of the remaining corners and sew on the marked line. Trim the excess

fabric away ¼" from the sewn seam and press. Keep all matching prints together. **Make 168** units. **2C**

3 block construction

Sew 2 rows of 2 matching units together as shown. Notice how each unit is positioned. **3A**

Sew the 2 rows together to complete the block. **Make 42**. **3B**

Block Size: 9½" unfinished, 9" finished

4 make horizontal sashing strips

Arrange 6 sashing rectangles and (5) 2½" cornerstone squares as shown. Sew the units in 1 long strip. Press towards the rectangles. **Make 6** horizontal sashing strips. **4A**

5 arrange & sew

Refer to the diagram on page 121 to lay out the blocks in **7 rows** with each row being made up of **6 blocks**. Place a sashing rectangle in between the blocks Sew the blocks and sashing rectangles together to form the 7 rows. Press the seams of each row towards the sashing rectangles. Place a horizontal sashing strip in between each row. Sew the rows and horizontal sashing strips together. Press the seams in 1 direction to complete the quilt center.

4A

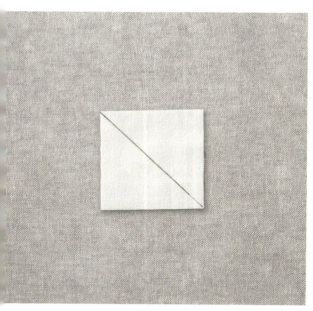

1   On the reverse side of each of the 2½″ background squares, draw a line from corner to corner once on the diagonal or press a crease in place to mark a sewing line.

2   Place a marked 2½″ background square on 2 opposite corners of a 5″ square with right sides facing. Sew on the marked line then trim ¼″ away from the sewn seams.

3   Place another 2½″ marked square on 1 of the remaining corners and sew on the marked line. Trim the excess fabric away ¼″ from the sewn seam and press. This makes 1 unit of the block. Make 4.

4   Sew 2 rows of 2 units together. Notice how each unit is positioned. Sew the 2 rows together to complete 1 block. Make 42.

5   Lay out the blocks in rows with a sashing rectangle between each block. Make sashing strips by sewing a sashing rectangle to a 2½″ cornerstone. Continue in this manner until you have sewn a strip made up of 6 sashing rectangles and 5 cornerstones.

6 inner border

Sew the remaining (8) 2½" background strips together end-to-end to make 1 long strip. Trim the inner borders from this strip.

Measure, cut, and attach the inner borders to the quilt top. The strips are approximately 75½" for the sides and approximately 68½" for the top and bottom.

7 outer border

Cut (8) 6" strips across the width of the fabric. Sew the strips together end-to-end to make 1 long strip. Trim the outer borders from this strip.

Measure, cut, and attach the outer borders to the quilt top. The strips are approximately 79½" for the sides and approximately 79½" for the top and bottom.

8 quilt & bind

See pages 18-25 for tips on finishing your quilt!

FALLING CHARMS

I have a quilt that I received as a gift years ago from a dear friend. I love that I can imagine her small, capable hands skillfully sewing every stitch. I love that the quilt represents the kindness and warmth I always feel when I'm with her. But if I'm being really honest, I don't actually love the look of the quilt. My style is a bit more modern: sleek and minimalist. And this old fashioned quilt just doesn't fit. Dusty mauves and mature florals in a traditional flower basket pattern would have been a perfect match for my grandma's house, but they look absolutely out of place in my more contemporary home. That's why I was thrilled to learn about the modern movement in quilting. It blends the generations-old tradition of quilting with the style of today. I have been able to take the skills I've learned over the years and combine them with my own sense of style to create quilts that really represent who I am.

Of course quilting style is as individual and varied as taste in fashion, art, or food. Ask one hundred quilters to identify the most beautiful quilt in the world and you will certainly get one hundred different answers. Some like bold colors, some muted. Some prefer busy, patterned fabrics, others like to stick with solids or simple motifs. Some cling to the time-tested designs of traditional quilting, and some love the style innovations of modern quilting.

My friend once asked me to describe modern quilting. As much as I love modern quilting, I wasn't exactly sure what to tell her. But since then I've decided that rather than being confined by one narrow definition, modern quilting can really be anything that branches out from tradition. That being said, there are a few characteristics that can be considered decidedly modern. One of the hottest trends in modern quilting is the use of solid fabrics. Solid fabrics are fun because they really allow the piecing to shine. The focus is all on color and shape. Solid fabrics also make a great canvas for creative stitching. Because of the simplicity of the fabric, the eye is drawn to details that might be missed with busier fabric.

Other common markers of modern quilting include large amounts of negative space, unexpected scale, and bold prints. Of course, a modern quilter may use all or none of these elements. The most important thing is, in modern quilting we should feel free to break from tradition and create something unique and beautiful that is all our own. After all, a quilt truly is a piece of art that reflects the aesthetic and imagination of the artist.

Whether you are a quilter that loves to experiment with new styles and methods or you prefer to stick to tradition, one thing is sure. Modern quilting has caused this wonderful artform to become attractive to a wider audience. Old craftsmanship can meld with new artistic ideas. Modern quilting allows tradition and innovation to be stitched together in new and wonderful ways.

MATERIALS

QUILT SIZE
82" x 95"

BLOCK SIZE
7" unfinished, 6½" finished

QUILT TOP
4 packages of 5" squares
1 roll of 2½" background strips
  (42" width of fabric)
1½ yards 42" wide matching
  background fabric - includes border

BINDING
¾ yard fabric

BACKING
8½ yards - vertcial seam(s)
  or 3 yards 108" wide

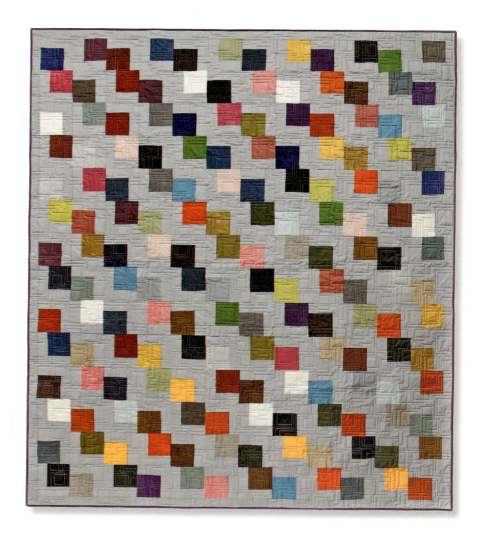

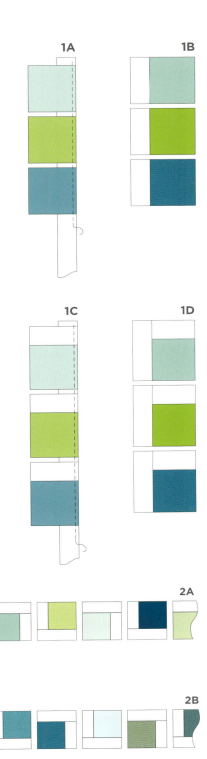

1A

1B

1C

1D

2A

2B

1 chain piece

We will use a chain piecing method to add 2½" background strips to 2 sides of our 5" squares. Lay a 5" square, right sides facing, on the top end of a background strip, and line up the right edges. Be sure the square is below any selvage of the strip. Using a ¼" seam allowance, sew the square to the strip. Take a few stitches and add another square in the same manner. Repeat to add the remaining squares to strips—8 squares to a strip. **1A**

Trim the background strip even with the top and bottom edges of each square. Open and press the seam allowances of each unit towards the square. **1B**

Rotate the units so that the background sections are at the top. Using the same chain piecing method, sew the units to the background strips, right sides facing, along the right edges. **1C**

As done previously, trim the background strip even with the top and bottom edges of the units. Open and press. **Make 168** blocks. **1D**

Block Size: 7" unfinished, 6½" finished

2 arrange & sew

Refer to the diagram on page 127 as necessary to arrange the blocks in **14 rows** with each row having **12 blocks.** The first row begins with a block positioned with the outer strips in the upper right corner. The next block is positioned so the strips are in the lower left corner. Alternate the blocks in this manner all across the row. **Make 7** odd-numbered rows and press the seam allowances toward the right. **2A**

Begin the second row with a block positioned with the outer strips in the lower left corner. The next block is positioned so the strips are in the upper right corner. Alternate the blocks in this manner all across the row. **Make 7** even-numbered rows and press the seam allowances toward the left. **2B**

Nest the seams and sew the rows together, beginning with an odd-numbered row and alternate with an even-numbered row, to complete the quilt center.

3 border

Cut (9) 2½" strips across the width of the border fabric. Sew the strips together end-to-end to make 1 long strip. Trim the borders from this strip.

Measure, cut, and attach the borders. The strips are approximately 91½" for the sides and approximately 82½" for the top and bottom.

4 quilt & bind

See pages 18-25 for tips on finishing your quilt!

1 Stitch 5″ squares to 2½″ background strips.

2 Trim off the excess fabric even with the 5″ squares.

3 Rotate the units so the background sections are at the top. Sew the units to the (2) 2½″ background strips.

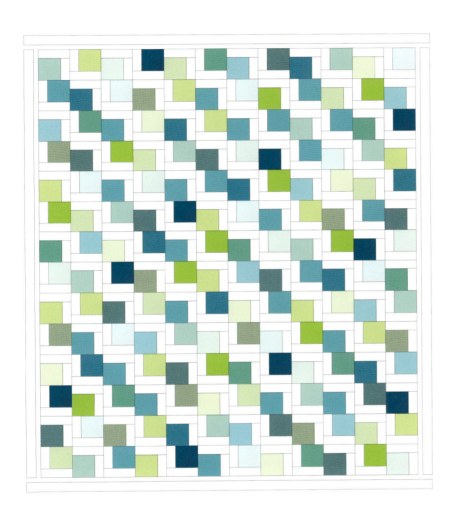

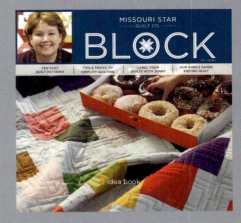

BLOCK
FUN FACT

DONUTS ON A QUILT!

"When deciding on the cover of our very first issue of BLOCK we liked a photo featuring the Falling Charms quilt. We thought it might look cute displayed with some donuts in a box on top and a hand reaching out to grab one of the donuts. When we conducted a poll to see which cover image we should use, we had such fun and interesting comments. We especially liked the ones that told us we should never put donuts on a quilt! So we ended up going with a different cover image. That's where it began. We have since featured plenty of unexpected things on quilts. We want to make sure we carry across the message that we use our quilts and love them until we have to make more—because those have been loved so well!"

—*Christine Ricks*

Stay Organized While Sewing

Think of a design wall as a bulletin board for organizing your quilts in progress. I like to stand back and see the whole project in front of my eyes, while sewing it together in short spurts. You can purchase a portable design wall or make your own with foam core insulation boards wrapped in quilt batting.

Imagine the scene. You've carefully selected and cut the fabrics, assembled the quilt blocks, and are just inches away from completing your quilt top. With a mighty sense of accomplishment, you shake out the wrinkles and admire your work. Then with a gasp, you realize you've entirely messed up the order of the blocks! Letting out a big sigh, you grab your trusty seam ripper and start fixing.

Most quilters can relate with this story, having mixed up the quilt blocks a time or two. But after spending time with so many quilting friends over the years, I've picked up some great tips for keeping blocks in the right order and orientation while you sew a quilt top. These quilt layout hacks will give you some ideas for how to keep the fabric pieces organized.

Design Wall

Here's one of the tools of the trade you never knew you needed until you had it. Think of a design wall as a bulletin board for organizing your quilts in progress. I like to stand back and see the whole project in front of my eyes, while sewing it together in short spurts. You can purchase a portable design wall or make your own with foam core insulation boards wrapped in quilt batting.

Creating a design wall for your quilts doesn't have to be expensive. A flannel-backed tablecloth will do the trick! Simply hang the tablecloth against the wall and use small nails or thumbtacks to secure in place. (Alternately, you can use a large piece of quilt batting.) The fuzzy fabric surface will grab on to your quilt blocks so you can arrange them and rearrange them to your heart's content. After sewing a few together, return the pieced blocks to the design wall and grab some loose ones. Tip: Before you rely on this method exclusively, make sure you've turned off any fans and closed the windows to keep pieces from blowing away. It's also a good idea to close the door to any children or pets who might rush in or out of the room!

Painter's Tape

Unlike masking tape, blue painter's tape won't leave a sticky residue on fabric and it's perfect for making your own block labels. After arranging your quilt blocks, assign each row a number. In the first row, label the blocks 1A, 1B, 1C, and so on. Repeat for the next row (2A, 2B, 2C…).
Tip: The orientation of a label is important. Keep the letters right side up to make sure you don't flip the blocks as you go. After the blocks are labeled, neatly stack the pieces in each row and secure with a binding clip. The block piles are ready to be assembled at the sewing machine or saved for a rainy day.

The orientation of a label is important. Keep the letters right side up to make sure you don't flip the blocks as you go. After the blocks are labeled, neatly stack the pieces in each row and secure with a binding clip.

Before joining any of the blocks, use your phone to take a quick photo of the quilt layout. Refer back to this photo as often as needed to make sure everything checks out! If one of your blocks falls off the design wall or a pin comes loose, refer back to that photo to for peace of mind.

Numbered Pins

Is it just me, or are flower head sewing pins better than chocolate? Aside from being downright cute, flower head pins can be used to make reusable quilt block markers. With a thin permanent marker, write a short identifier on each pin's head (1A, 1B, 1C...2A, 2B, 2C). Keeping the blocks in rows, slip a pin into the center of each block, making note of the orientation. Stack the blocks in each row and transfer them to the sewing machine to be joined. Carefully remove the sewing pins from each block and you can save them for your next labeling project.

If you don't have flower head pins, you can purchase lettered quilt block markers and use regular sewing pins to attach them. Another tip is label quilt blocks using plastic bread bag ties or paper merchandise tags, both of which have a small hole in the top that's perfect to stick a pin in.

Take A Photograph

None of these labeling methods are foolproof, so it helps to use them in combination with my secret weapon—a photo. Before joining any of the blocks, use your phone to take a quick photo of the quilt layout. Refer back to this photo as often as needed to make sure everything checks out! If one of your blocks falls off the design wall or a pin comes loose, refer back to that photo for peace of mind.

Sticky Notes, Plastic Bags and File Folders

If you tend to work on quilt blocks one row at a time, you can raid your home for office supplies to help you keep them organized. Sticky notes can be used to label stacks of blocks, with or without directional arrows to guide you through confusing layouts. Place ready-to-sew blocks in plastic sandwich bags or freezer bags. The plastic bags can then go into file folders which are neatly labeled with the quilt name and date. For smaller quilts with large blocks, you may wish to skip the labeling all together and lay out pieces on the table or floor right next to the sewing machine, for a pick-up-and-go approach.

Whatever system you choose for keeping your quilt layout in check, make sure you follow through. And if you do make a mistake, remember that we've all been there. Take a deep breath, and reach for that seam ripper. It's all sew-ing to be okay!

LUCKY PENNY

Find a penny, pick it up. All day long you'll have good luck! Create a charming Lucky Penny quilt from easy half-hexagons and your luck is sure to change for the better. Hexagons are known for being a little tough to quilt, but we've simplified these classic shapes by splitting them in half for easy piecing. We promise you won't have to sew a single Y-seam! So, grab two packages of your favorite 5″ squares, add on two more packages of complementary background squares, and it's your lucky day!

MATERIALS

QUILT SIZE
45½" x 57"

QUILT TOP
2 packages 5" print squares
2 packages 5" background squares

BORDER
½ yard

BINDING
½ yard

BACKING
3 yards - horizontal seam(s)

OTHER
Missouri Star Small Half Hexagon
Template for 5" Charm Packs
& 2½" Jelly Rolls

1 cut

Set (12) 5″ print squares aside for another project.

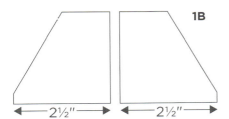

1A

Stack as many print squares as you are comfortable cutting at once on your cutting surface. Carefully cut the squares in half once to create (2) 5″ x 2½″ rectangles from each. Use the template to cut half-hexagons from each rectangle. Keep matching print pairs together. You will need a **total of 72** pairs of half-hexagons. **1A**

1B

←——2½″——→   ←——2½″——→

In the same manner, cut 2 half-hexagons from each of the 5″ background squares. Subcut 26 of the half-hexagons in half to make quarter-hexagons. You will need a **total of 142** background half-hexagons and a **total of 52** background quarter-hexagons. **1B**

2 arrange & sew

Select 18 pairs of print half-hexagons, 30 background half-hexagons, and 12 quarter-hexagons. Layout the half-hexagons in **6 rows** of **11 half-hexagons** as shown in the diagram below. Be sure the matching print half-hexagons line up along their longest sides. Begin and end each row with a quarter-hexagon. **2A**

Starting at 1 end of the row, match the slanted sides right sides facing, offset the 2 pieces at the ¼″ seam line, and sew together. Continue adding the pieces together to form the rows. Press the seams of the odd-numbered rows to the right and the even-numbered rows to the left. Nest the seams and sew the rows together to complete 1 section. Repeat to **make 4** sections.

Sew the 4 sections together, as shown in the diagram on page 137. Notice that sections 2 and 4 are rotated 180°.

Sew 11 background half-hexagons together in a row. Sew a quarter-hexagon to each end to complete the row. **Make 2**. **2B**

Sew a row of the background half-hexagons and quarter-hexagons to the top and bottom to complete the quilt center.

2A

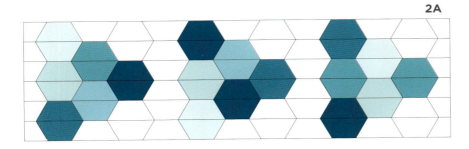

2B

1   Cut the 5" squares in half once to create (2) 5" x 2½" rectangles. Use the template to cut half-hexagons from each rectangle.

2   Join the half-hexagons along their slanted edges. Once the seam is sewn and pressed to 1 side, they will form a straight row.

3   Cut 26 background half-hexagons in half to yield 52 background quarter-hexagons.

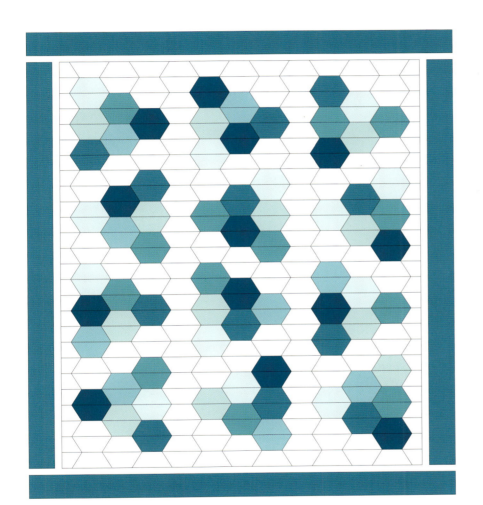

3 border

Cut (5) 3″ strips across the width of the border fabric. Sew the strips together end-to-end to make 1 long strip. Trim the borders from this strip.

Measure, cut, and attach the borders. The strips are approximately 52½″ for the sides and approximately 46″ for the top and bottom.

4 quilt & bind

See pages 18-25 for tips on finishing your quilt!

PERIWINKLE

This antique pattern was discovered on a fateful day when two sisters walked into Missouri Star. They brought in a couple of gorgeous quilts their mother had made which inspired this quilt design. Because it was handmade with tricky Y-seams, we updated it with easy piecing papers and our handy Periwinkle template to help it come together in no time at all. Now you can stitch it up yourself and recreate this lovely vintage pattern. You'll need two packages of 5″ squares along with 3¾ yards of background fabric to begin. All of this is thanks to those two sweet sisters who shared their wonderful heirloom quilts with us.

MATERIALS

QUILT SIZE
58" x 70"

BLOCK SIZE
12½" unfinished, 12" finished

QUILT TOP
2 packages 5" print squares
3¾ yards background fabric

BORDER
1 yard

BINDING
¾ yard

BACKING
3¾ yards - horizontal seam(s)

ADDITIONAL SUPPLIES
1 package Small Wacky Web
   Triangle Paper Refills
1 Missouri Star Small Periwinkle
   (Wacky Web) Template for
   5" Charm Packs
Glue Stick - optional

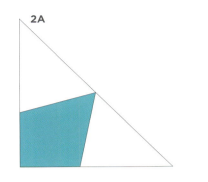

2A

1 cut

Select (80) 5″ squares from the 2 packs. Using the template, cut 1 shape from each. (There will be 4 squares left over for another project.)

From the background fabric, cut (20) 6½″ strips across the width of the fabric. Subcut the strips into 5″ x 6½″ rectangles for a **total of 160.**

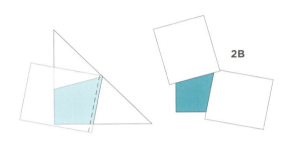

2B

2 block construction

Each block is made up of 4 triangular units. If you are using the glue stick, add a dab of glue to the reverse side of a print periwinkle shape. Place the shape on top of a paper triangle in the corner with the right side of the fabric facing up. If you are not using a glue stick, pin the shape to the paper triangle. **2A**

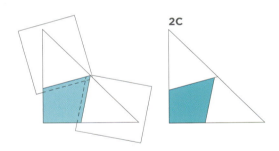

2C

Align the edge of a background rectangle with the edge of the periwinkle shape with right sides facing. Sew in place, using a ¼″ seam allowance. Repeat for the other side of the triangle. **2B**

Press the triangle unit. Turn over and trim the excess fabric evenly with the triangle paper. **Make 4** per block. **2C**

2D

Lay out 4 triangle units. Remove the paper and sew the units together to complete 1 block. **Make 20. 2D**

Block Size: 12½″ unfinished, 12″ unfinished

3 arrange & sew

Lay out the blocks in rows with each row having **4 blocks. Make 5 rows.** Press the seam allowances of the even-numbered rows toward the left and the odd-numbered rows toward the right. This will make the seams nest and the corners match more easily.

Sew the rows together to complete the center of the quilt.

4 border

Cut (6) 5½″ strips across the width of the fabric. Sew the strips together end-to-end to make 1 long strip. Trim the borders from this strip.

Measure, cut, and attach the border to the quilt top. The strips are approximately 60½″ for the sides and approximately 58½″ for the top and bottom.

5 quilt & bind

See pages 18-25 for tips on finishing your quilt!

1 Use the template to cut periwinkle shapes from 5″ print squares.

2 Place the periwinkle shape on top of a paper triangle in the corner with the right side of the fabric facing up.

3 Align the edge of a background rectangle with the edge of the periwinkle shape with right sides facing. Sew in place using a ¼″ seam allowance.

4 Add another rectangle to the other side of the periwinkle shape and sew in place as before.

5 Trim each section evenly with the paper.

6 Sew 4 periwinkle sections together to complete the block.

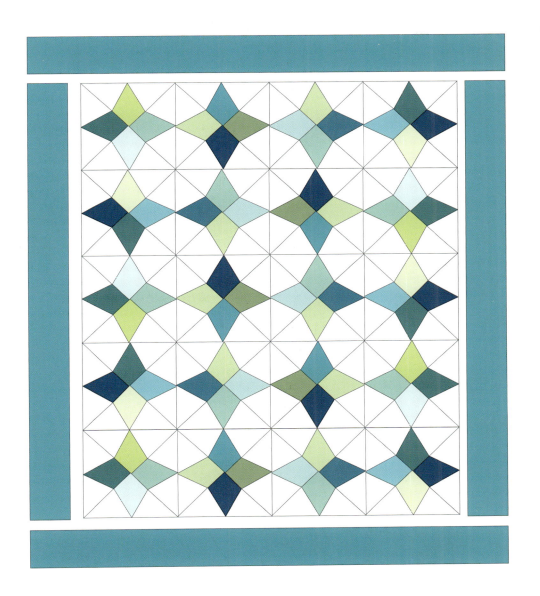

HAPPY LITTLE HOUSES

I had my entire life mapped out by the tender age of thirteen. Armed with a wealth of knowledge gathered from my favorite fantasy novels and Disney movies, I created an image of the perfect fairytale life, complete with a castle, a glittering tiara, and the most gallant of knights in shining armor.

I was sure that someday I would live in a charming little yellow house with a white picket fence that wrapped all the way around a flawlessly manicured lawn. My family would always be smiling, dinner would always turn out to be delicious, and the laundry would always be folded. As a part of this fantasy world, I even picked out the perfect married name to complete the fantasy: Jenny Livingston.

It's true, I didn't actually know a single soul with the last name of Livingston. There was no dreamy Livingston boy down the street. I just thought that "Jenny Livingston" had a nice, classy ring to it. I remember spending many long hours in my biology class doodling "Jenny Livingston" again and again in my notebook. I developed quite the elegant signature for my imaginary adult self!

Well, quite a few years have gone by and, not surprisingly, those dreams never did come to pass. No yellow house, no "Jenny Livingston," not even the tiara! But as I look back over the years, I am filled with gratitude for the beautiful life I do have. How could any perfect yellow house even begin to compare with the wonderful experiences I have shared with my husband and our seven children? Thank goodness life never really does go according to plan! Dreaming about the future is a pleasant distraction, but I think the secret to finding your real happily ever after is as simple as traveling along the road of life and finding joy in whatever comes your way.

This darling Happy Little Houses quilt is filled with an entire neighborhood of the cutest houses you've ever seen. Each one is unique and filled with love. No matter where you live, or what your family looks like, love is what makes a house a home.

MATERIALS

QUILT SIZE
56" x 65"

BLOCK SIZE
4½" x 10½" unfinished,
4" x 10" finished

QUILT TOP
3 packages 5" print squares
½ yard navy solid fabric
2¼ yards light blue solid fabric
  - includes blue sashing

SASHING
¾ yard coordinating green
  print fabric

BINDING
¾ yard

BACKING
3½ yards - horizontal seam(s)

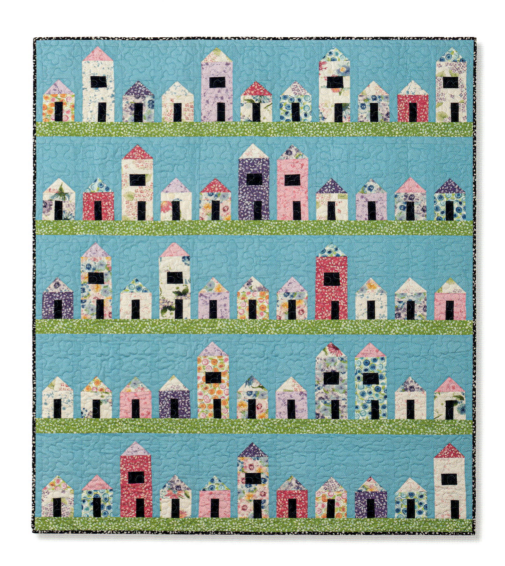

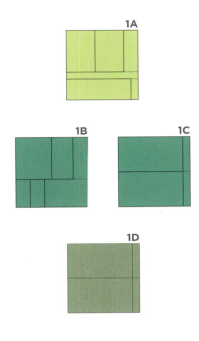

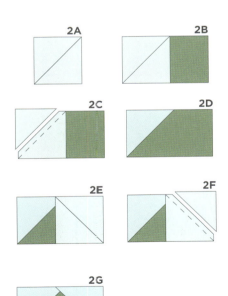

1 cut

Note: If the green print fabric you chose is also included in your packages of 5″ print squares, you might choose to set those squares aside for another project.

Select (39) 5″ print squares to use for the small houses. From each selected square, cut:

- (1) 3″ strip across the width of the square. Subcut (2) 3″ x 2″ rectangles from the strip.

- (1) 1½″ strip across the width of the square. Subcut (1) 1½″ x 4½″ rectangle from the strip. Keep the 3 rectangles together in a set. You will have a **total of 39** sets of small house rectangles. **1A**

Select 16 pairs of matching 5″ print squares to use for the tall houses.
- From 1 square in each pair:
  - (1) 3″ strip across the width of the square. Subcut (1) 3″ x 2½″ rectangle and (1) 3″ x 1½″ rectangle from the strip.

  - The remaining portion of the square should be a 2″ strip. Subcut the 2″ strip into (2) 2″ x 1½″ rectangles. **1B**

- From the second matching square in each pair, cut:
  - (2) 2½″ strips across the width of the fabric. Subcut a 2½″ x 4½″ rectangle from each of the strips. **1C**

  Keep the 6 rectangles together in a set. You will have a **total of 16** sets of tall house rectangles.

Select (28) 5″ print squares to use for the roofs. Cut each selected square in half horizontally to yield 2 rectangles. Trim each rectangle to 4½″ x 2½″. A **total of (55)** 4½″ x 2½″ rectangles are needed. Set all remaining print squares aside for another project. **1D**

From the navy solid fabric:
- Cut (2) 3″ strips across the width of the fabric. Subcut 3″ x 1½″ rectangles from the strips. Each strip will yield up to 28 rectangles and a **total of (55)** 3″ x 1½″ rectangles are needed.

- Cut (1) 2″ strip across the width of the fabric. Subcut a **total of (16)** 2″ x 2½″ rectangles from the strip. Set the remainder of the fabric aside for another project.

From the light blue solid fabric:
- Cut (5) 5″ strips across the width of the fabric. Subcut 5″ x 4½″ rectangles from the strips. Each strip will yield up to 9 rectangles and a **total of (39)** 5″ x 4½″ rectangles are needed.

- Cut (7) 2½″ strips across the width of the fabric. Subcut 2½″ squares from the strips. Each strip will yield up to 16 squares and a **total of (110)** 2½″ squares are needed.

Set the remaining fabric aside for the sashing.

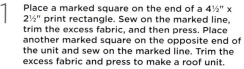

1 Place a marked square on the end of a 4½" x 2½" print rectangle. Sew on the marked line, trim the excess fabric, and then press. Place another marked square on the opposite end of the unit and sew on the marked line. Trim the excess fabric and press to make a roof unit.

2 Sew a 3" x 2" print rectangle to both long edges of a navy solid rectangle and then press. Sew the matching 1½" x 4½" print rectangle to the top of the unit and press towards the top.

3 Sew a roof unit to the top of the house unit and press. Sew a 5" x 4½" light blue solid rectangle to the top and press towards the top to complete the small house block. Make 39 small house blocks.

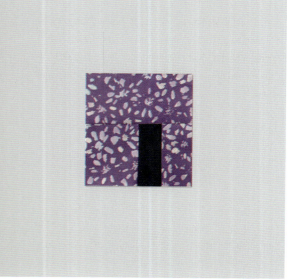

4 Sew a 3" x 2½" print rectangle to the left side of a 3" x 1½" navy solid rectangle and press. Sew matching 3" x 1½" print rectangle to the right side of the unit and press. Sew a matching 2½" x 4½" print rectangle to the top and press to create the door unit.

5 Sew the matching 2" x 1½" print rectangles to the short sides of the 2" x 2½" navy solid rectangle and press. Sew the matching 2½" x 4½" print rectangle to the top and press.

6 Sew a roof unit to the top of the window unit and press. Sew the door unit to the bottom and press to complete the tall house block. Make 16 tall house blocks.

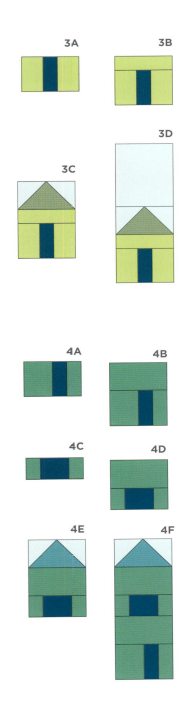

2 make roof units

Mark a diagonal line once corner to corner on the reverse side of each 2½" light blue solid square. **2A**

Place a marked square on top of a 4½" x 2½" print rectangle as shown, right sides together. **2B**

Sew on the marked line and then trim the excess fabric ¼" from the sewn seam. Press towards the corner. **2C 2D**

Place another marked square on top of the unit as shown, right sides together. **2E**

Sew on the marked line and then trim the excess fabric ¼" from the sewn seam. Press towards the corner to complete the roof unit. **Make 55** roof units and then set them aside for now. **2F 2G**

3 make small house blocks

Pick up 1 set of small house rectangles, (1) 3" x 1½" navy solid rectangle, 1 roof unit, and (1) 5" x 4½" light blue solid rectangle. Make sure the roof unit does not match the set of small house rectangles you chose.

Sew the 3" x 2" print rectangles to the long edges of the navy solid rectangle. Press the seams towards the darker fabric. **3A**

Sew the 1½" x 4½" print rectangle to the top edge of the unit. Press the seam towards the top. **3B**

Sew the roof unit to the top of the house and press the seam towards the bottom. **3C**

Sew the 5" x 4½" light blue solid rectangle to the top of the unit. Press the seam towards the top to complete the block. **Make 39** small house blocks and set them aside for now. **3D**

Block Size: 4½" x 10½" unfinished, 4" x 10" finished

4 make tall house blocks

Pick up 1 set of tall house rectangles, 1 roof unit, (1) 3" x 1½" navy solid rectangle, and (1) 2" x 2½" navy solid rectangle.

Sew the 3" x 2½" print rectangle to the left side of the 3" x 1½" navy solid rectangle. Press the seam towards the darker fabric. Sew the 3" x 1½" print rectangle to the right side of the navy rectangle. Press the seam towards the darker fabric. **4A**

Sew 1 of the 2½" x 4½" print rectangles to the top of the unit and press the seam towards the top. We'll refer to this as the door unit for clarity. The door unit can be set aside for a moment. **4B**

Sew the 2" x 1½" print rectangles to the short sides of the 2" x 2½" navy solid rectangle. Press the seams towards the darker fabric. **4C**

Sew the remaining 2½" x 4½" print rectangle to the top of the unit. Press the seam towards the top. We'll call this the window unit for clarity. **4D**

Sew the roof unit to the top of the window unit. Press the seam towards the bottom. **4E**

BLOCK FUN FACT

OUR FIRST PHOTOSHOOT

"I have so many good memories of our Block journey. We've had to learn it all and make it up along the way. I'll never forget the first photo shoot that we had. Alan and I flew to Salt Lake City to meet Christine, Block's Creative Director, and the photo team. It was just magical to me. Christine had this detailed shot list, there were props, and every picture just looked so beautiful. I knew we could make quilts, but that weekend I knew our little magazine was going to be one of a kind!"

—Natalie Earnheart

Pick up the door unit you placed aside earlier and sew it to the bottom. Press the seam towards the bottom to complete the block. **Make 16** tall house blocks and set them aside for now. **4F**

Block Size: 4½" x 10½" unfinished, 4" x 10" finished

5 make sashing

From the light blue solid fabric, cut (22) 1½" strips across the width of the fabric.

- Subcut 15 of the strips into 1½" x 10½" rectangles. Each strip will yield 4 rectangles and a **total of 60** are needed. We'll refer to these as the sashing rectangles for clarity.

- Sew the 7 remaining 1½" strips together to form 1 long strip. Set this strip aside for the moment.

From the green print fabric, cut (7) 2½" strips across the width of the fabric. Sew the strips together to form 1 long strip. Set this strip aside for the moment.

6 arrange & sew rows

See the diagram on the next page to arrange the blocks in **5 rows** each made up of **11 blocks**. When you're happy with the arrangement, place a sashing rectangle in between each block and on both ends of each row. Sew the blocks and sashing rectangles together to form the rows. Press the seams towards the sashing rectangles.

After the rows are complete, measure the length of the rows. They should measure approximately 56½". Pick up the long strips of light blue solid and green print fabrics. Cut 5 horizontal sashing rectangles to the length of your rows.

Sew a light blue solid horizontal sashing rectangle to the top of each row and press the seam towards the top. Sew a green print horizontal sashing rectangle to the bottom of each row and press the seam towards the bottom. Sew the rows together and press the seams towards the bottom to complete the quilt top. **6A**

7 quilt & bind

See pages 18-25 for tips on finishing your quilt!

6A

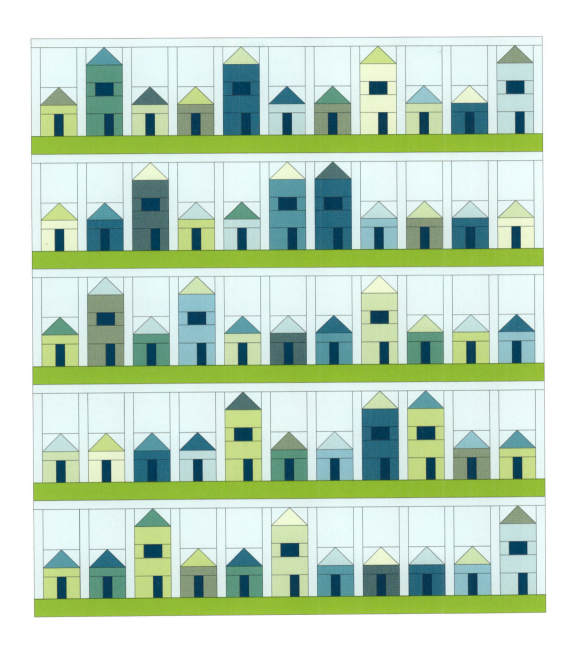

JACOB'S LADDER

There's a reason they call the classics the "oldies, but goodies." There's a certain timeless characteristic that touches folks over generations. That's true in literature, music, film, art, and, we might add, quilts. Jacob's ladder is just one of those classics. And this remixed classic is updated with quick piecing tricks that will make it a goodie just for you! It's easily created with quick four-patch units and simple half-square triangles. When they're all pieced together in a quilt top, an intriguing ladder design appears on the diagonal. Don't you want to see where it leads?

MATERIALS

QUILT SIZE
72" x 76"

BLOCK SIZE
4½" unfinished, 4" finished

QUILT TOP
5 packages of 5" light squares
5 packages of 5" dark squares

BINDING
¾ yard

BACKING
4¾ yards - vertical seam(s)
   or 2½ yards of 108" wide

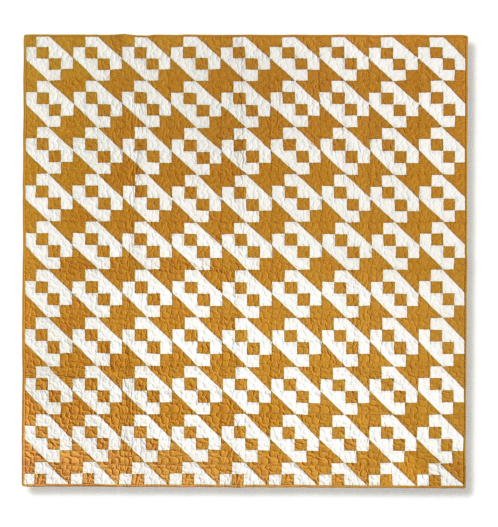

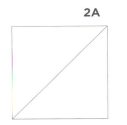
2A

1 half-square triangles

Mark a line from corner to corner on the diagonal of each of (86) 5″ light squares. **2A**

Place a marked light square atop a 5″ dark square with right sides facing. Sew on both sides of the marked line using a ¼″ seam allowance. Cut on the marked line. Open each unit and press the seam toward the dark fabric. Trim the units to 4½″ square. Repeat with the remaining 85 light squares paired with 85 dark squares. Each set of sewn squares will yield 2 half-square triangles and a **total of 171** are needed. **Note**: You will have 1 half-square triangle left over. **2B**

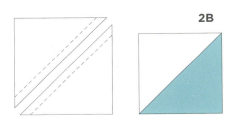
2B

Block Size: 4½″ unfinished, 4″ finished

2 make 4-patches

Layer a light square atop a dark square with right sides facing. Sew down 2 opposite sides of the square with a ¼″ seam allowance. Measure 2½″ from either sewn edge and cut the sewn squares in half vertically. Open and press toward the dark fabric. **3A**

3A

Layer the 2 pieces together with right sides facing. The light portion should be touching the dark portion. Sew down the 2 sides of the strip units perpendicular to the seams. Again measure 2½″ from either sewn edge and cut the sewn squares in half. Open to reveal (2) 4-patch units.

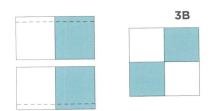
3B

Press. Repeat with the remaining dark and light squares to make a **total of (171)** 4-patches. **Note**: You will have (1) 4-patch left over. **3B**

Block Size: 4½″ unfinished, 4″ finished

3 arrange & sew

Refer to the diagram on page 157 as necessary to lay out your units in **19 rows** of **18 blocks**. Notice that the blocks alternate between 4-patches and half-square triangles in each row. The 4-patches are all oriented exactly the same throughout the quilt but the half-square triangles change direction. Sew the blocks together in rows. Press the seam allowances of all odd-numbered rows to the left and all even-numbered rows to the right. Nest the seams and sew the rows together. Press to complete the center of the quilt top .

4 quilt & bind

See pages 18-25 for tips on finishing your quilt!

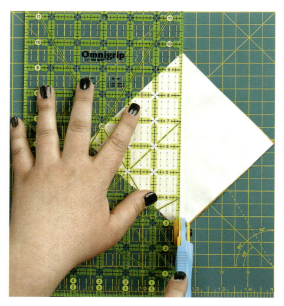

1 After sewing on either side of the marked center, cut between stitching lines. Yield: 2 half-square triangles.

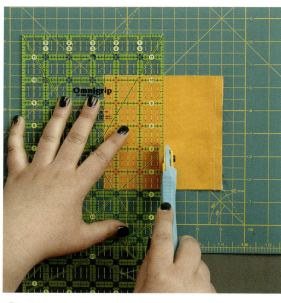

2 After sewing on 2 opposing outside edges, cut the squares in half between the seams.

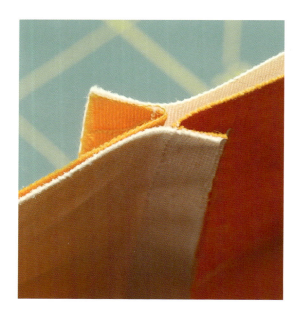

3 An easy way to nest your seams is to press to the dark side. This will allow the seams to naturally come together. Also, you can take the 2 middles and rub with your fingers to feel them align.

4 Again, cut down the middle between the 2 seams.

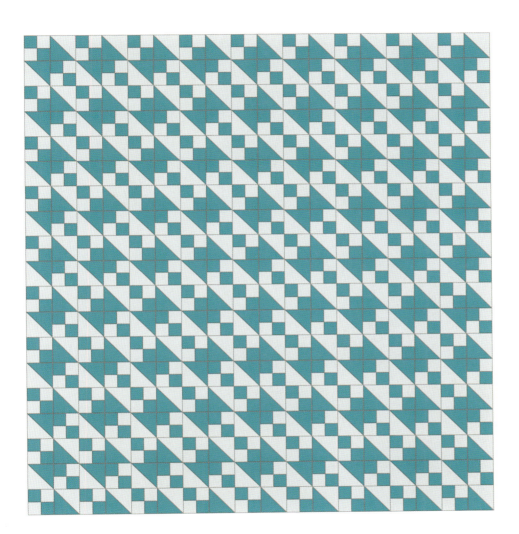

FAKE CHRISTMAS

"My family had so much fun getting together in early November to have a 'fake Christmas' photoshoot for our first holiday issue of Block. That year we made all of our favorite traditional foods and got everyone dressed up for family photos. The kids had so much fun pretending. We wrapped up some empty boxes and when the photoshoot was over Misty's son, Ezra, wanted to open them. He opened the first box and shouted out, 'An iron, I got an iron!' He was so excited about it, and his sweet, innocent gratitude was perfect. We joked that Jake and Misty should add one to his real Christmas list. There are so many more fun family things that we have had the opportunity to do together, that I can't list them all, but it has been so meaningful for us to get together and document some of our best traditions and happiest moments."

—*Natalie Earnheart*

Size it Up or Size it Down: Adapting Quilt Patterns

Quilt patterns aren't exactly one-size fits all. Sometimes you find the perfect quilt pattern, but it's too small for your bed. Or maybe it's too big to finish in time for a last-minute gift. Or maybe you've even run out of fabric! Well, have no fear! Here are five simple ways to change the size of your quilt, and the process is simpler than you might think. From adding borders and sashing to changing the size of your precuts, these solutions make sizing up or down a snap.

Add Borders

Perhaps the easiest way to gain inches on your quilt top is to add a border around it. Borders can enhance the look of a pieced quilt by framing it in. Depending on your aesthetic, you may like to piece borders from precut squares or yardage of a single fabric. If your quilt already has a border, you could even increase the width or add a second border for contrast.

Since there are no hard or fast rules about border sizes, you can make them as wide as you want. A 14" border is going to look more at home on a king-size quilt than a twin, for example. Use your design sense to keep borders in proportion and you'll be just fine! When framing in a bed quilt with a border, you'll also want to keep in mind the size of the mattress you're trying to cover. If the original quilt matches the mattress's dimensions, an added-on border should hang nicely off the bed.

Add Rows and Columns

To keep the integrity of a quilt design intact while upsizing, one option is to add extra blocks of the same size. Piecing enough blocks to gain one extra row and one additional column will often get you to your goal size (e.g. queen to king). Since you aren't changing the size of the blocks, it should be relatively easy to purchase extra precuts and grow your quilt kit to the next size up.

Want a really easy way to make your pieced blocks go the distance? Add solid setting squares in a checkerboard pattern to stretch out the blocks you have. Sure this will change the look of the quilt, but you just might love the results. Consult your design wall!

Make Blocks Larger

Ready to test those math skills? Increasing the size of your blocks is another way to upsize a quilt top. This will be easier with some blocks than others. For instance, numerous charts calculate half-square triangles from different size fabric squares,

Want a really easy way to make your pieced blocks go the distance? Add solid setting squares in a checkerboard pattern to stretch out the blocks you have. Sure this will change the look of the quilt, but you just might love the results. Consult your design wall!

Using a different sized precut is a simple way to adjust the size of a quilt. You can make a Jacob's Ladder quilt using the instructions found on page 152 and a different sized precut to create a much bigger or much smaller sized quilt.

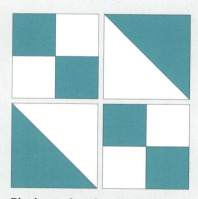

Block made using 2½" squares

Each 4-patch and half-square triangle should be squared up to 1½" and finish at 1". A quilt laid out in 19 rows of 18 blocks would measure 18" x 19".

Blocks made using 5" squares

Each 4-patch and half-square triangle should be squared up to 4½" and finish at 4". A quilt laid out in 19 rows of 18 blocks would measure 72" x 76".

Blocks made using 10" squares

Each 4-patch and half-square triangle should be squared up to 9½" and finish at 9". A quilt laid out in 19 rows of 18 blocks would measure 162" x 171".

Disappearing Hourglass 2 Quilt as found on page 32.

Finished quilt measures: 79" x 90".

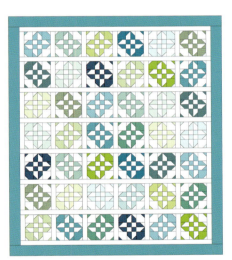

Disappearing Hourglass 2 Quilt adding 2½" sashing with no change to block sizes or border widths.

Finished quilt measures: 89" x 102"

but resizing a log cabin requires new calculations for each layer and could be more work than you bargained for. When the math works, upsizing blocks is a great option for quilters. Grab a calculator and pencil and experiment. Wouldn't it be magical to turn a lap quilt pattern into a king quilt by doubling the block size? Think of all the time you'd save by churning out big blocks from 10" squares instead of 5" charms!

Add Sashing

Some quilt patterns look sharp with sashing added in between blocks. Sashing changes the overall look of your quilt, but you can audition the blocks first by placing them on a design wall and squinting. Or, try taking a photo from far away! Be careful not to go too wide with the sashing, or it could detract from the beautifully pieced blocks.

Use a quilt calculator or quilt design software to figure out how much yardage to cut for extras like sashing and borders. When increasing the size of your quilt, make sure to jot down each measurement. For bonus points, you can make a cutting chart for extra pieces and draw out the new quilt diagram on graph paper. When drawn to scale, this adjusted quilt layout can help you decide how much extra yardage to put in your cart for sashing, borders, and binding.

Sizing Down

It often makes sense to size a pattern down rather than up. For a quick finish (with fabric to spare!), it's perfectly acceptable to turn a larger quilt into a smaller size. Before you make any decisions, you can sketch your quilt layout on graph paper. How does the layout look after striking a row or column? If the appearance is to your liking, you can simply sew fewer blocks to make a smaller quilt.

Otherwise, you may choose to narrow the sashing or borders to lose inches off your quilt—or eliminate them completely. You can also experiment with making the block size smaller. In any case, you won't need to purchase additional fabric when you size down a quilt, but do the math ahead of time so you know how much less fabric to buy.

COMMON QUILT SIZES

Crib: 45" x 60"

Lap: 60" x 72"

Twin: 72" x 96"

Queen: 108" x 96"

King: 120" x 120"

Cal King: 120" x 130"

Handmade quilts can vary in size, but this list of common quilt sizes will give you a rough estimate of the dimensions, give or take a few inches on either side.

ALL MY LOVE

Express your love with a wall hanging featuring four half-square triangle hearts. It's absolutely adorable and incredibly easy to make. We all enjoy a good love story and this one is a romance we're all familiar with: a timeless tale of a quilter who loved some pretty fabric and made it into a gorgeous quilt! This wall hanging is created with easy half-square triangles arranged into four heart shapes. The story begins with three packages of 2½" print squares or one charm pack, and ½ yard of background fabric. Every time you see it, you'll fall in love all over again!

MATERIALS

QUILT SIZE
31½" x 31½"

BLOCK SIZE
9½" unfinished, 9" finished

QUILT TOP
3 packages 2½" print squares*
½ yard background fabric
 - includes sashing

BORDER
¾ yard

BINDING
½ yard

BACKING
1¼ yards

*Note: You can replace the 3 packages of 2½"
print squares with 1 package of 5" print squares.
Simply cut the 5" squares in half both vertically
and horizontally to yield 2½" squares before
beginning the pattern.*

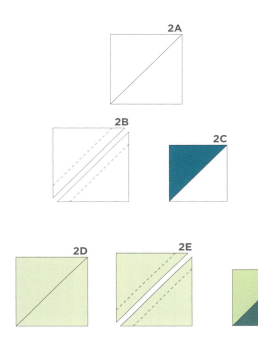

2A

2B

2C

2D

2E

2F

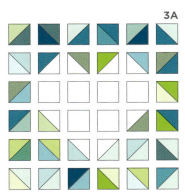

3A

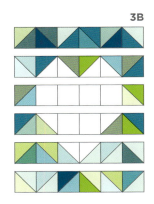

3B

1 cut

From the background fabric:

- Cut (1) 2½" strip across the width of the fabric. Subcut a **total of (16)** 2½" squares from the strip.

- Cut (2) 2" strips across the width of the fabric. Subcut each strip into 2" squares. Each strip will yield up to (20) 2" squares and a **total of 24** squares are needed.

- Set the remainder of the fabric aside for the sashing.

2 half-square triangles

Mark a diagonal line on the reverse side of (16) 2½" background squares. **2A**

Lay a marked background square atop a 2½" print square, right sides facing. Sew on both sides of the marked line with a ¼" seam allowance. **2B**

Cut on the marked line and open each unit to reveal 2 half-square triangles. Press each unit towards the darker fabric. **2C**

Repeat the previous steps using an additional (15) 2½" print squares and the 15 remaining marked background squares. You will have a **total of 32** print/background half-square triangles.

Select (44) 2½" print squares. Mark a diagonal line on the reverse side of each of the selected squares. **2D**

Select another (44) 2½" print squares. Lay a marked print square atop an unmarked

print square, right sides facing, and sew on both sides of the marked line with a ¼" seam allowance. Cut on the marked line and open each unit to reveal 2 half-square triangles. Press each unit towards the darker fabric. **2E 2F**

Pair each of the remaining marked print squares with an unmarked print square and repeat the previous instruction to create half-square triangles. You will have a **total of 88** print/print half-square triangles.

Trim all half-square triangles to 2".

Note: You'll need to save (9) 2½" print squares for the cornerstones, so don't put them aside just yet.

3 block construction

Select 8 print/background half-square triangles, 22 print/print half-square triangles, and (6) 2" background squares. Arrange them in **6 rows** of **6 units**, as shown in the diagram. **3A**

Sew the units together to form rows. Press the seams of the odd-numbered rows towards the left and the seams of the even-numbered rows towards the right. **3B**

Nest the seams and sew the rows together. Press the seams towards the bottom to complete the block. **Make 4** blocks. **3C**

Block Size: 9½" unfinished, 9" finished

1 Mark a line once on the diagonal on the reverse side of a 2½" background square. Lay the marked square on top of a print square, right sides facing. Sew on both sides of the marked line with a ¼" seam allowance. Cut on the marked line.

2 Open both units and press the seam allowance towards the darker fabric. Repeat to make 32 background/print half-square triangle units. Trim all units to 2".

3 Mark a line once on the diagonal on the reverse side of a 2½" print square. Lay the marked square on top of another print square, right sides facing. Sew on both sides of the marked line with a ¼" seam allowance. Cut on the marked line.

4 Open both units and press the seam allowance towards the darker fabric. Repeat to make 88 print/print half-square triangle units. Trim all units to 2".

5 Arrange 8 background/print half-square triangles, 22 print/print half-square triangles, and (6) 2" background squares in 6 rows of 6, as shown.

6 Sew the units together to form rows. Press the seams of the odd-numbered rows towards the left and the seams of the even-numbered rows towards the right. Nest the seams and sew the rows together. Press to complete the block.

4 make horizontal sashing strips

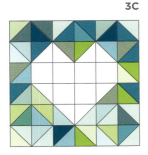

3C

Select (9) 2½" print squares and set the rest of the print squares aside for another project. Trim the selected squares to 2".

From the background fabric, cut (3) 2" strips across the width of the fabric. Subcut each strip into 2" x 9½" sashing rectangles. Each strip will yield 4 sashing rectangles and a **total of 12** are needed.

Pick up 3 of the 2" print squares you trimmed earlier. Arrange the 3 squares and 2 of the sashing rectangles into a row. Sew the pieces together and press the seams towards the background rectangles. **Make 3** horizontal sashing strips. **4A**

4A

5 arrange & sew

Refer to the diagram below to lay out the blocks in **2 rows** made up of **2 blocks**. Place a 2" x 9½" sashing rectangle in between each block and on both ends. Sew the blocks and sashing rectangles together to form the rows. Press the seams of each row towards the sashing rectangles.

Place a horizontal sashing strip in between the 2 rows and on the top and bottom. Sew the rows and horizontal sashing strips together. Press the seams towards the bottom to complete the center of the quilt top.

6 border

From the border fabric, cut (4) 5" strips across the width of the fabric. Trim the borders from these strips.

Measure, cut, and attach the border to the quilt top. The strips are approximately 23" for the sides and approximately 32" for the top and bottom.

7 quilt & bind

See pages 18-25 for tips on finishing your quilt!

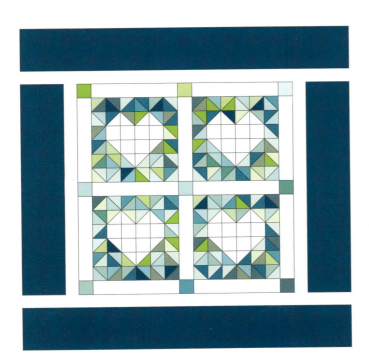

HALF-SQUARE HARMONY BAG

Are you a quilter on the go? Create this charming Half-Square Harmony Bag and you can tote a cute quilt along with you wherever you roam. This generously-sized bag is perfect for toting your odds and ends and it's made with a slew of easy half-square triangles. Create a sturdy strap, add a lining and you're done! All you need to make it is one package of 5" print squares and 1 yard of coordinating fabric for the strap and lining. Stitch it up and you'll be sew stylish!

MATERIALS

PROJECT SIZE
16" x 20"

BLOCK SIZE
4½" unfinished, 4" finished

PROJECT SUPPLIES
1 package 5" print squares
1 yard coordinating print
   - includes strap & lining
25½" x 40" scrap of batting

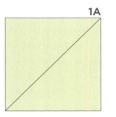
1A

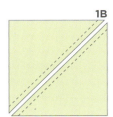
1B

1C

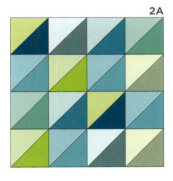
2A

2B

1 make half-square triangles

Separate your package of 5″ print squares into lights and darks. You'll need at least 16 lighter squares and 16 darker squares. You can put the rest of the 5″ squares in your package aside for another project.

Mark a diagonal line once corner to corner on the reverse side of each of the 16 light squares. **1A**

Lay a marked square on top of a dark print square, right sides facing. Sew on both sides of the diagonal line with a ¼″ seam allowance. Cut on the marked line. **1B**

Open each half-square triangle and press the seam allowances towards the darker fabric. **1C**

Repeat with all remaining squares for a **total of 32** half-square triangles. Trim all half-square triangles to 4½″.

2 make the bag exterior

From the coordinating print, cut a 4½″ strip across the width of the fabric. Subcut (2) 4½″ x 16½″ rectangles from the strip. Set the rest of the fabric aside for now.

Arrange the half-square triangles in **4 rows** of **4 blocks** as shown. The lighter print of each half-square triangle should be oriented in the upper left corner of each block. When you're happy with your arrangement, sew the blocks together to form rows. Press the seams of the odd-numbered rows to the left and the seams of the even-numbered rows to the right. Nest the seams and sew the rows together. Press the seams towards the bottom. **Make 2**. **2A**

Sew a 4½″ x 16½″ coordinating print rectangle to the bottom of each unit. Press the seam towards the bottom. **2B**

From the batting, cut a 1½″ strip across the width of the batting. Subcut a 1½″ x 40″ rectangle and set this rectangle aside for the strap. Cut the remainder of the batting in half to yield (2) 20″ x 24″ rectangles.

Lay each pieced rectangle on top of a 20″ x 24″ batting rectangle and quilt, using any design you like. Trim and square up the edges of both exterior panels.

Place the template found on page 172 a bottom corner of an exterior panel and trace along the curved edge of the template. Repeat for both bottom corners on each exterior panel. Cut each of the corners along the traced curved lines. **2C**

Lay 1 exterior panel on top of the other, right sides facing. Sew around the 2 sides and the bottom edge. Clip the curved seams and set this aside for the moment. **2D**

3 make the bag lining

From the coordinating print, cut a 20½"
strip across the width of the fabric and set
the rest aside for now. Subcut (2) 20½" x
16½" lining rectangles. Place the template
found to the lower right on a bottom
corner of a lining rectangle and trace
around the curved edge of the template.
Repeat for both bottom corners on each
lining rectangle. Cut each of the corners
along the traced curved lines.

Lay 1 lining rectangle on top of the other,
right sides facing. Sew around the 2 sides
and the bottom edge, but leave a 4"
opening for turning in 1 of the side seams.
Clip the curved seams. **3A**

4 make the strap

From the coordinating print, cut a
5" strip across the width of the fabric.
Subcut a 5" x 40" rectangle from the strip.
Set the remainder of the fabric aside for
another project.

Fold the 5" x 40" print rectangle in half
lengthwise, wrong sides together. Press.
Reopen the rectangle and then press both
long raw edges in about ½" towards the
center, wrong sides together. Be sure you
have nice, hard creases at this point. Tuck
the 1½" x 40" batting rectangle under the
folded edge of the fabric strip. **4A**

Once the batting is tucked inside, refold
along the creases and topstitch about
¼" from each edge. Add another line of

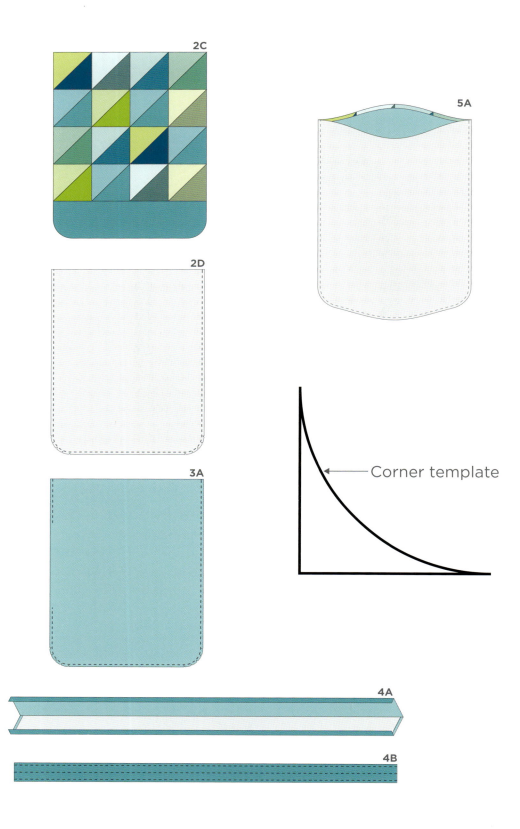

Corner template

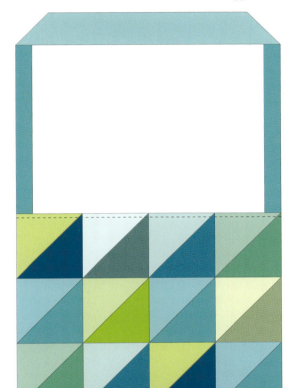

5B

topstitching down the center of the fabric to create the strap. **4B**

Trim the strap to your desired length.

5 finish the bag

Keep the bag exterior inside out. Place the strap inside and center 1 end off the strap to the sewn seam allowance on 1 side of the bag and pin or clip in place. Repeat for the other end of the strap. Be sure your strap is not twisted and then pin or clip it to the opposite side of the bag.

Turn the bag lining right side out. Drop the lining into the exterior. The right sides of the bag exterior and lining should be touching each other. Align the side seam allowances and pin or clip the exterior, lining, and strap in place in several places. **5A**

Start at a side seam and sew all of the way around the bag's top edge using a seam allowance a bit wider than ¼".

Reach into the bag and find the opening that was left in the side seam of the lining. Pull the whole bag through the opening to turn it right side out. After turning, whipstitch the opening in the lining closed and tuck it inside the bag. Topstitch around the top edge of the bag about ¼" from the edge to complete. **5B**

HALF-HEXI SNOWMAN

Stitch up a wintry table runner featuring a couple of precious half-hexagon snowmen that won't turn into puddles when the weather gets warmer! You can leave them out as long as you'd like and they'll make your winter tablescape cozy as-can-be. And you don't need a single snowball to bring them together; they're created with a few 5″ squares in assorted prints and accessories made from scraps to create a top hat, carrot nose, and coal eyes. If you have leftover precuts from previous projects, this is the perfect opportunity to use them up!

MATERIALS

TABLE RUNNER SIZE
19" x 45"

TABLE RUNNER TOP
9 *pairs* of matching 5" print squares
(1) 5" dark print square
1 scrap of black for buttons, mouths,
  and eyes - approximately 4" x 7"
1 scrap of orange for noses
  - approximately 2" x 3"
½ yard white solid

SASHING, BORDER, & BINDING
¾ yard dark print

OTHER
2½" x 17" rectangle of fusible web
Missouri Star Large Half Hexagon
  Template for 10" Squares

BACKING
1½ yards

1A

1 cut

From the white solid, cut (2) 4¾" strips across the width of the fabric. Using the template, subcut half-hexagons from each trip for a **total of 8** half-hexagons. **1A**

Set 1 pair of the lightest 5" print squares and the 1 dark print square aside for the moment.

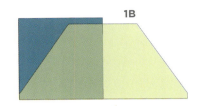

1B

From each of the remaining 8 matching pairs of 5" print squares, cut quarter-hexagons. Lay 1 matching pair of 5" dark print squares on top of each other, right sides facing and all edges aligned on your cutting surface. Lay the template on top of the squares, lining up the bottom corner and the center marks of the template with the side edges of the squares. **1B**

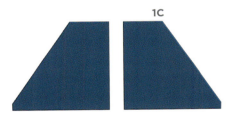

1C

Cut a pair of quarter-hexagons from the squares. Each pair of matching squares will yield a right quarter-hexagon and a left quarter-hexagon. Repeat with the remaining pairs of 5" print squares to **make 8** sets of matching quarter-hexagons. **1C**

2A

Set the remaining 5" dark print square and 2 matching light print squares aside for the moment.

Using the templates found on page 179, trace 2 noses, 4 eyes, and 12 button/mouth pieces onto the paper side of the fusible web. Roughly cut around the shapes. Following the manufacturer's directions, adhere the nose shapes to the scrap of orange fabric and the eyes and

2B

mouth/button shapes to the scrap of black fabric. Cut out the shapes along the traced lines and set them aside for the moment.

From the border fabric, cut (1) 1½" wide strip—subcut this strip into (2) 1½" x 14" rectangles. Set the remaining fabric aside for the borders.

2 sew

Select a set of matching quarter-hexagons. Sew a quarter-hexagon to either side of a white half-hexagon. Repeat to **make 8** snowman units and set them aside for the moment. **2A**

Sew a 5" light print square to either side of the 5" dark print square to **make 1** center strip unit. **2B**

3 arrange & sew

Lay out the snowman units, the center strip unit, and the dark print rectangles as shown. **3A**

Stitch the pieces together and press.

Referring to the diagram on page 179, position the appliqué pieces onto the snowmen as shown. Once you are happy with the placement, adhere each shape in place following the manufacturer's directions. Use a zigzag or blanket stitch around each piece to appliqué in place.

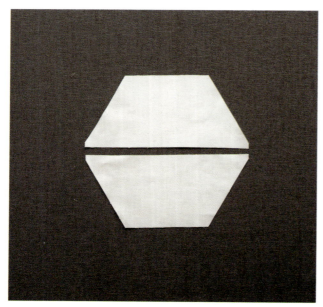

1   Use the template to cut a total of 8 half-hexagons from the white solid fabric.

2   Lay a pair of matching 5" print squares right sides together. Use the template to cut quarter-hexagons from the squares and separate them to reveal 2 quarter-hexagons with symmetrical angles.

3   Sew a quarter-hexagon to either side of a white half-hexagon. Make 8.

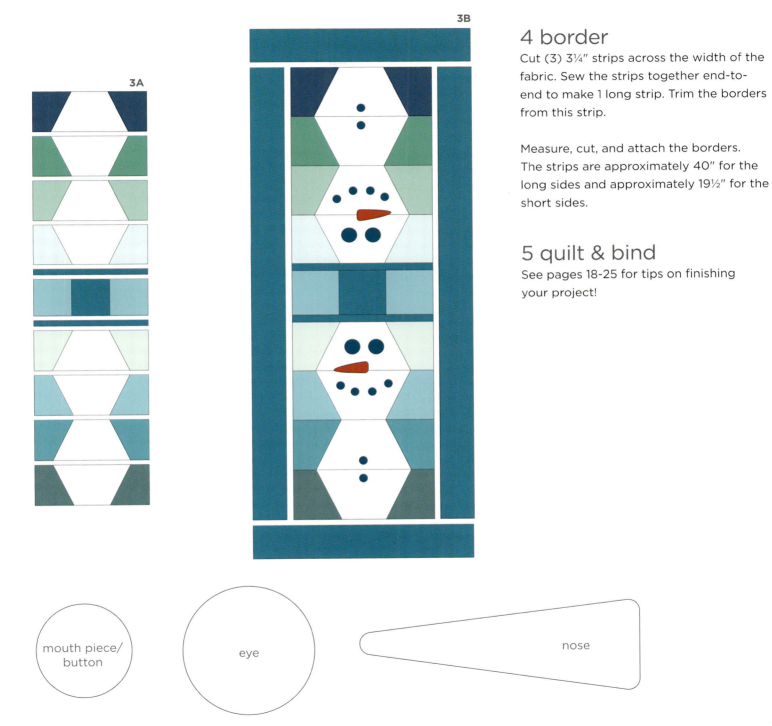

3A

3B

4 border

Cut (3) 3¼" strips across the width of the fabric. Sew the strips together end-to-end to make 1 long strip. Trim the borders from this strip.

Measure, cut, and attach the borders. The strips are approximately 40" for the long sides and approximately 19½" for the short sides.

5 quilt & bind

See pages 18-25 for tips on finishing your project!

mouth piece/
button

eye

nose

Journal

Discover more about what inspires you to quilt as you delve into your inner designer with this section of journal prompts. When you realize how you like to create, it can help you become a better quilter. We can't wait to see what you come up with next! Share your latest creations with us at **#msqcshowandtell.**

1 WHY DO YOU QUILT? WHAT PROMPTED YOU TO START QUILTING?

2 WHAT IS THE EASIEST QUILT YOU'VE EVER MADE? WHAT IS THE HARDEST QUILT YOU'VE EVER MADE? DID YOU ENJOY MAKING ONE MORE THAN THE OTHER?

3 IF YOU HAD TO MAKE THE SAME QUILT OVER AND OVER, WHICH QUILT WOULD IT BE?

Quilt Planner

Use this easy quilt planner to help you design your next creation. From the fabrics to the pattern, it's all up to you! Sketch your quilt design out using the handy grid below and you can even color it in. How fun! Then, you'll have a reminder of your design process to look back on in the future.

PROJECT IDEA _____

_____

_____

FABRICS _____

_____

COLORS

PRECUTS USED _____

_____

_____

YARDAGE _____

BLOCK DESIGN

SIZE _____ **X** _____

SKETCH   _SIZE_ _____ **X** _____

NOTES _____

_____

_____

_____

_____

_____

_____

_____

Build Your Own

Use this space to sketch or draw your own design based on the patterns in this section.

PRECUT GUIDE
2½" STRIPS | 2½" x Width of Fabric
typically 40 strips in a package

How many packs do I need?
1 = Lap/Twin
2 = Queen
3 = King

Make your own precut of 2½" strips
3 yards for a total of various fabrics required.

How many prints come in a precut?
16 - 24

Tip for Working with Precuts
Precut sizes can vary slightly. Yes, precuts are cut to measure, however, depending on the manufacturer, the size of the precut may be measured from the outer peak of the pinked edge or the inner valley of the pinked edge, or it may not have a pinked edge at all. This may cause some variation in sizes. Before you combine precut packs, measure them to see what the differences are between them, but don't trim them down. Just decide which edge will be your guide and get stitching!

How many ways can you cut up a 2½" strip?
(Measurements based on 42" usable fabric. Width of individual fabrics may vary.

(2) 2½" x 21" rectangles

(4) 2½" x 10" rectangles

(8) 2½" x 5" rectangles

(17) 2½" x 2½" squares

2½"

STRIPS

We've gathered up a few of our favorite 2½" strip quilt patterns for the Best of BLOCK to show you just how versatile they are. Strips used to be seen only as borders or sashing in between blocks but here they're the star of the show! Don't be shy, get your hands on as many jelly rolls as you dare and get stitching with these quick and easy quilt patterns. In no time at all, you'll be relaxing with a quilt you made yourself! Keep on reading and learn how to make the most of this delightful precut. Get stitching and let the good times roll!

DESERT SUNSET

You may think it's a mirage that's causing this stunning quilt pattern to seem so simple, but we assure you, it really is that easy! You'll love how quickly this quilt comes together using blocks made from strip sets. All you have to do is unroll a pack of 2½" strips and sew them together in sets of five strips. Then, they're divided into squares, cut twice on the diagonal, and reassembled to create a sensational design. When you're all through, set off on a roadtrip through the desert at twilight with this cozy quilt in tow.

MATERIALS

QUILT SIZE
59" x 59"

BLOCK SIZE
13½" unfinished, 13" finished

QUILT TOP
1 roll of 2½" x 42" strips

OUTER BORDER
¾ yard

BINDING
½ yard

BACKING
3¾ yards - vertical seam(s)

1 make strip sets

Sew 5 assorted strips together to make 1 strip set. **Make 8.** Cut each strip set into (4) 10½" squares. Stack the matching squares together. **1A**

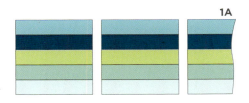

2 sew

Layer 2 matching squares together with right sides facing. The strips on 1 of the squares need to be vertical while the strips on the other square need to run horizontally. **2A**

Note: Make sure your squares are always oriented in the same direction, otherwise your blocks may not match.

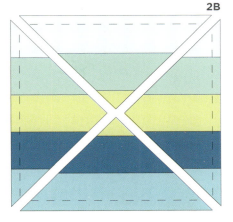

Sew all the way around the perimeter of the squares using a ¼" seam allowance. Cut the sewn square from corner to corner twice on the diagonal. Open to reveal 2 sets of 2 matching block units. Repeat to make a **total of 16** sets of 4 matching units. **2B 2C**

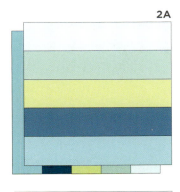

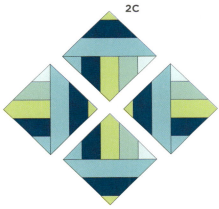

Lay out 4 matching units and stitch them together to complete 1 block. **Make 16** blocks. **2D**

Block Size: 13½" finished, 13" finished

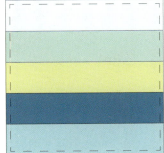

3 arrange & sew

Lay out the blocks in **4 rows** with each row having **4 blocks.** Sew each row together and press the seam allowances in the odd-numbered rows toward the right and the even-numbered rows toward the left. Nest the seams and sew the rows together. Press the seams toward the bottom to complete the quilt center.

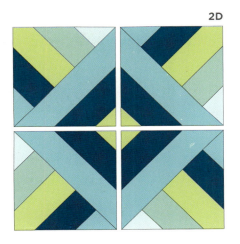

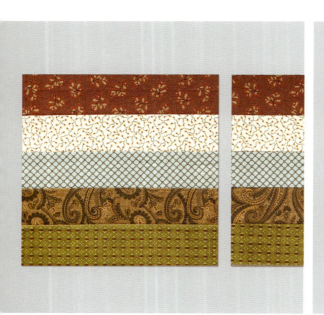

1 Sew 5 assorted strips together to make 1 strip set. Cut each strip set into (4) 10½″ squares. Stack the matching squares together.

2 Layer 2 matching squares together with right sides facing. The strips of 1 of the squares should run vertically and the other horizontally.

3 After sewing all the way around the perimeter of the squares using a ¼″ seam allowance, cut the sewn squares twice on the diagonal. Open to reveal 2 sets of 2 matching units.

4 Lay out 4 matching units and stitch them together to complete 1 block.

5 Lay out the blocks in rows of 4. When you are happy with the appearance, sew the rows together.

4 border

Cut (6) 4″ strips across the width of the fabric. Sew the strips together end-to-end to make 1 long strip. Trim the borders from this strip.

Measure, cut, and attach the borders to the quilt top. The strips are approximately 52½″ for the sides and approximately 59½″ for the top and bottom.

5 quilt & bind

See pages 18-25 for tips on finishing your quilt!

BINDING TOOL STAR

I've made a quilt or two in my day, as you well know, and I love to have a few tips and tricks up my sleeve to make things easier. But quilting has a learning curve and, just like everybody else, my skills still needed to catch up with my enthusiasm right at the beginning. Now, you might laugh when I tell you that when we opened our first quilt shop, I didn't exactly know how to finish off a quilt binding correctly. I had read about it over and over and I just couldn't figure it out.

For me, I enjoy learning from a real live person instead of a book. So, when I went to quilt market and I saw a woman doing demonstrations of the perfect binding finish, I went right up to her and asked, "Would you do that again? One more time? Can I film this?" Luckily that woman happened to be the fabulous Susan Brown and she just went along with it. We still have the tutorial on our YouTube channel!

Ever since that day when Susan (who is now a treasured employee of Missiouri Star and our retreat coordinator) was so patient and helpful to me, she has become a great friend. When I saw that she had used her incredible Binding Tool to make a star quilt, I loved the idea right away. Of course, I went right home and tried it for myself, using her star as inspiration.

Next, I turned to my ingenious teenage grandson, Noah, who took off and came up with a whole quilt design for Susan's star. I get so energized when I see what other quilters are doing, but even those who have never made a quilt can be amazing sources of inspiration as well. I love this quilt because it reminds me that I can do great things when I rely on great friends. They say it takes a village to raise a child, and in my opinion it's the best way to make a quilt too!

MATERIALS

QUILT SIZE
77" x 77"

BLOCK SIZE
16½" unfinished, 16" finished

QUILT TOP
1 roll 2½" print strips
2¾ yards background fabric
   - includes inner border

PIANO KEY BORDER
1 package 5" print squares

BINDING
¾ yard

BACKING
4¾ yards—vertical seam(s)
   or 2½ yards 108" wide

OTHER
The Binding Tool by TQM Products

1 cut & sort

1A

From the 2½" print strips, select 8 each of 4 different values: dark, medium, medium-light and light. Keep the strips folded in half.

1B

From each folded 2½" print strip, cut out 2 Binding Tool shapes and (1) 2½" x 5" rectangle.

Tip: To fit all of the shapes on a folded strip, the Binding Tool can be turned 180° to cut the second shape. **1A**

Each strip will yield 2 pairs of Binding Tool shapes—1 left-angled and 1 right-angled shape in each pair, plus (2) 2½" x 5" rectangles.

Group sets of 1 angled pair of each of the 4 color values. **Make 16** sets. **1B**

Set the remaining print strips aside for another project.

Set (1) 5" print square aside for another project. Cut each remaining 5" print square in half to create (2) 2½" x 5" rectangles from each. Add these to your previously cut rectangles for a **total of (146)** 2½" x 5" print rectangles. Set these aside for the piano border.

From the background fabric, cut:

- (4) 8⅞" strips across the width of the fabric. Subcut each strip into (4) 8⅞" squares. Subcut each of these squares in half on the diagonal to create a **total of (32)** 8⅞" triangles.

- (4) 8½" strips across the width of the fabric. Subcut each strip into (4) 8½" squares, for a **total of (16)** 8½" background squares.

- (4) 2½" strips across the width of the fabric. Subcut each strip into (16) 2½" squares for a **total of (64)** 2½" background squares for the cornerstones.

- Set the remainder of the background fabric aside for the inner border.

2 block construction

Take 1 set of 4 angled pairs. Using a ¼" seam allowance, sew a 2½" cornerstone to the blunt end of each left-angled shape to make an angled unit. Press towards the cornerstone. **2A**

2A

Add a light right-angled shape to an 8½" background square as shown. Press toward the square. **2B**

2B

Select a same-print angled unit and add it to the bottom of the unit, as shown, nesting the seams as you sew. **2C**

2C

Continue in this fashion adding 4 prints—light to dark to both sides of the square. **2D**

2D

Attach an 8⅞" background triangle to either side of the block. Make dog ears at the ¼" seam allowance. Press towards the outside. Repeat with the remaining sets to **make 16** blocks. Square each block to 16½." **2E**

2E

Block Size: 16½" unfinished, 16" finished

1 Select (1) 8½" square and 1 light-colored right-angled shape. Match the long side of the shape to the square and sew right sides together.

2 Attach a solid cornerstone to the blunt end of all left-angled shapes, right sides together.

3 Attach the second shape with its cornerstone to the adjacent side of the square and sew. Nest seams. Continue in this fashion until 4 cornerstones have been added to the block.

4 Attach the (2) 8⅞" triangles to either side of the block. Square up to 16½."

3 arrange & sew

Arrange the blocks into **4 rows** of **4 blocks** as shown in the diagram below. Sew the blocks together to form the rows. Press the seams of the odd-numbered rows to the right and the seams of the even-numbered rows to the left. Sew the rows together to complete the center of the quilt.

4 inner border

From the remainder of the background fabric, cut (7) 2½" strips across the width of the fabric. Sew the strips end-to-end to create 1 long strip. Trim the borders from this strip.

Measure, cut, and attach the inner borders to the quilt top. The strips are approximately 64½" for the sides and approximately 68½" for the top and bottom.

5 piano key border

Pick up the 2½" x 5" print rectangles set aside earlier. Piece (34) 2½" x 5" rectangles together along the long edges, so that no 2 similar prints are touching. Press all the seams in the same direction. **Make 2**.

Measure the quilt top height and cut the pieced borders to that size. They should be approximately 68½" long. Attach to either side of the quilt. Press towards the inner border.

Repeat the same process, but use 39 rectangles for each top and bottom border. Measure and cut the borders to size. They should be approximately 77½" long. Attach and press towards the inner border.

6 quilt & bind

See pages 18-25 for tips on finishing your quilt!

Color Value: Choosing Fabrics with Confidence

As quilters, we instinctively know the value of fabric. We hoard it, pet it, stack it up in pretty piles, and photograph it. It's valuable, for sure! But understanding color value ... now that's another story. I used to agonize over my quilts, trying to match fabrics for hours, only to have the final outcome seem a little bland. I have learned since then that when it comes to color, it's about much more than matching. Color value goes deeper, exploring the way lights and darks play off of each other to create a pleasing color palette that will make your designs pop!

What is Color Value?

In the simplest terms, a fabric's color value is its lightness or darkness. When comparing two colors, the lighter color has a higher value, and the darker color has a lower value. For example:

pale pink = high value
navy blue = low value

Why Value Matters

Fabrics come in lights, mediums, and darks. When you use two dark-value fabrics to piece hourglass blocks, for example, it's harder to see the design. But if you use both light and dark fabrics, it gives your quilt blocks greater contrast and makes the hourglass pattern easier to see.

Just like with individual blocks, the whole quilt can start to look boring if you select fabrics of the same value. Picture a courthouse steps quilt top without any contrast. This classic quilt design relies on both low and high value fabrics to create a secondary pattern between blocks. Without the right placement of lights and darks, the quilt loses its visual punch.

Paying attention to color value allows you to create wonderful visual patterns in a quilt top. Alternate high- and low-value blocks for a checkerboard effect. Place all the light blocks toward the top, medium blocks in the middle, and dark blocks toward the bottom for an ombré effect. Or switch up the look every other row for a striped or wavy pattern.

Even when you use different colors of fabric, it's important to consider the value of each. For example, chocolate brown and burnt orange are both darker versions of their respective hues. For patchwork that pops, choose a creamsicle-colored orange, which is lighter, to pair with a darker brown. The contrast between high- and low-value colors will animate the design and draw your eye to the patchwork. If you prefer a more serene quilt top with piecing that blends together, you can pick fabrics of a similar value—all light, all medium, or all dark.

Determining Color Value

It's easy to determine the value of white and black fabrics. You can

The contrast between high and low-value colors will animate the design and draw your eye to the patchwork. If you prefer a more serene quilt top with piecing that blends together, you can pick fabrics of a similar value—all light, all medium, or all dark.

low-value

high-value

Pull out your cell phone and turn on the camera. With the color setting on black and white, look through the viewfinder. You should now be able to clearly see the lighter and darker fabrics in each group. Arrange all the fabrics from light (high-value) to dark (low-value) using the camera trick.

probably arrange grays from lightest to darkest with no trouble. But reds, greens, and blues? Many quilters find it challenging to determine lightness or darkness when dealing with fabrics from their stash.

If you want to practice, try this exercise, choose a dozen fat quarters and arrange them into three groups: light, medium, and dark tones. Now, within each group, try to sort the prints from lightest to darkest. Having a hard time? Pull out your cell phone and turn on the camera. With the color setting on black and white, look through the viewfinder. You should now be able to clearly see the lighter and darker fabrics in each group. Arrange all the fabrics from light (high-value) to dark (low-value) using the camera trick. Then turn off the camera to see how you did. Any surprises?

Another trick for finding color value is to wear color value finder glasses, which come with red, green, or blue lenses. You can also hold up a sheet of green or red plastic for the same effect. When viewing your fabric through a colored filter, you can sort lights from darks more easily, and choose the best colors for your project. **Note:** If you already have a lot of dark reds in your quilt, don't use the red filter, but choose a blue or green one instead.

If all else fails, try squinting at your fabrics. Ask yourself which colors

pop out at you, like a bright yellow, and which colors fade into the background, which will help you arrange fabrics by color value when no tools are available. With practice, you'll get better at seeing colors and choosing fabrics will get easier.

Design Tips

When planning your next quilt, remember that effective color placement is a powerful tool to improve your overall design. Here is some general advice on color and contrast as it relates to art.

- **High-contrast designs tend to excite the viewer, while low-contrast images are more calming.**

- **The human eye is naturally drawn to a light object against a dark background. The difference in values creates a focal point.**

- **Gradations of color (an ordered arrangement of lights, mediums, and darks) will create depth and dimension in your quilt top.**

With your newfound knowledge of color value in fabrics, try this assignment. Take a photo of a quilt from your past. Now, turn it black and white. Do you notice how value plays into the overall design? How would you improve on your fabric selections if you had it to do again?

JELLY ROLL RACE 3

Are you ready for a jelly roll race? Geared up? Helmet on? Well, maybe not helmet but, are your needles sharp? Bobbins filled? Machine oiled? Iron hot? Get ready. Get set. Quilt! A jelly roll race is a great way to spend an afternoon when you're in need of a quilt top right away or you just need a little excitement! This design is a fun, new twist on the traditional Jelly Roll Race with cute triangle dividers in between each strip. All you need to start is a roll of your favorite 2½" strips and 1 yard of background fabric and you're off to the races!

MATERIALS

QUILT SIZE
66½" x 79"

QUILT TOP
1 roll of 2½" print strips
1 yard background fabric
  - includes inner border

OUTER BORDER
1¼ yards

BINDING
¾ yard

BACKING
5 yards – vertical seam(s)
  or 2½ yards 108" wide

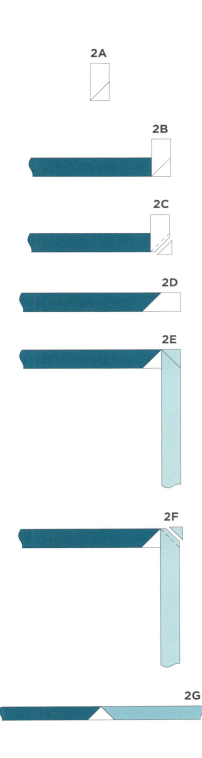

2A

2B

2C

2D

2E

2F

2G

1 cut

From the background fabric, cut (5) 2½" strips across the width of the fabric. Subcut into 2½" x 4½" rectangles. Each strip will yield at least 8 rectangles and a **total of 39** background rectangles are needed. Set the remaining fabric aside for the inner border.

2 make 1 long strip

Mark a 45° diagonal line on reverse side of each background rectangle, as shown, either by folding and pressing a crease or using a fabric pen. **2A**

Remove selvages from the ends of all the print strips.

Place a marked background rectangle on the end of a print strip, as shown, right sides facing. **2B**

Sew on the drawn line. Trim the excess fabric ¼" away from the sewn seam. **2C**

Press the seam allowance toward the print strip. **2D**

Lay another print strip on the background end of the pieced strip, as shown, right sides facing. Mark a 45° diagonal line from the top left of the strip either by folding and pressing a crease or using a fabric pen. **2E**

Sew on the drawn line. Trim the excess fabric ¼" away from the sewn seam. **2F**

Press the seam allowance toward the print strip. **2G**

Continue in this manner to add background rectangles and all of the remaining strips on 45° diagonals to make 1 long strip.

Cut 18" off the end of the strip. This ensures the triangles will not end up on the edge of the quilt center.

3 sew

Pick up both ends of the long strip. Lay 1 end on top of the other, right sides together. Sew the strip to itself *lengthwise* all the way back to the fold. Don't worry about twisting.

When you are close to the end, cut the fold, undoing any twist, and finish sewing the 2 strips together.

Layer the ends of the 2-strip set right sides together and repeat sewing lengthwise. Cut the fold and finish sewing the 4-strip set. Continue sewing the strips together in this fashion 5 times until your width is a **total of 32** strips. Press. Square to approximately 52" x 64½".

Note: Depending on the length of your strips, your quilt center width may differ a few inches from 52". Trim the width to your preference and make the appropriate adjustments to your borders.

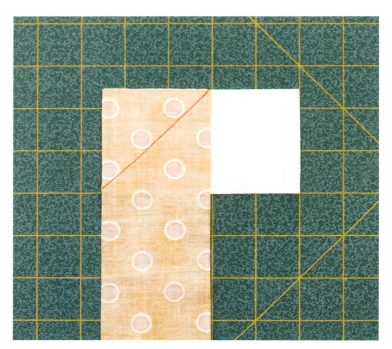

1 Alternate view of first seam. Use whichever view makes more sense to you.

2 Trim away the excess fabric.

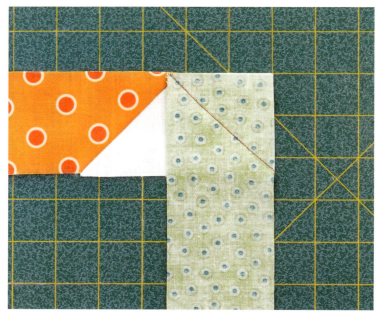

3 Add the next strip. It aligns to the top and right side of the white rectangle. The seam runs top left to bottom right.

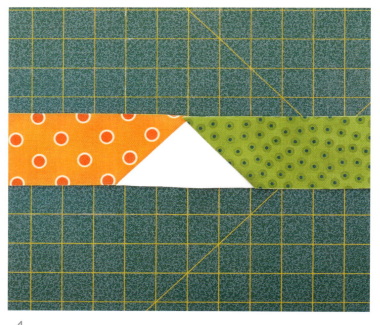

4 Trim the excess ¼" away from the sewn seam and press the strip open.

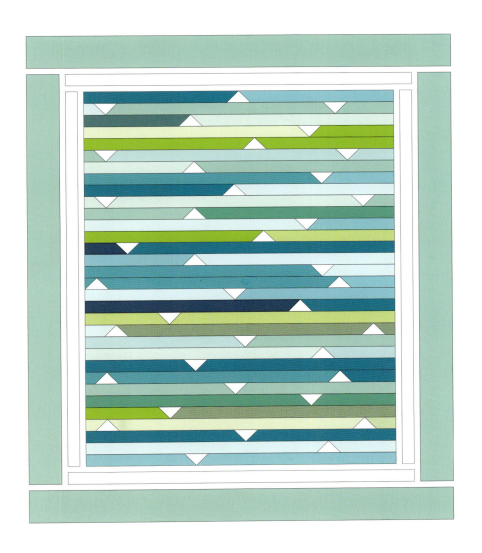

4 inner border

Cut (6) 2½" strips across the width of the inner border fabric. Sew the strips together end-to-end to make 1 long strip. Trim the border from this strip.

Measure, cut, and attach the inner border to the quilt top. The strips are approximately 64½" for the sides and approximately 56" for the top and bottom.

5 outer border

Cut (7) 6" strips across the width of the outer border fabric. Sew the strips together end-to-end to make 1 long strip. Trim the border from this strip.

Measure, cut, and attach the outer border to the quilt top. The strips are approximately 68½" for the sides and approximately 67" for the top and bottom.

6 quilt & bind

See pages 18-25 for tips on finishing your quilt!

PIECE OUT

I always dreamed of having a big family. Visions of endless picnics and games of backyard kickball were fulfilled when I was blessed with seven energetic children. I loved the snuggles, the laughter, and even some of the mischief. I did not, however, love the laundry.

In all my idyllic daydreams, I never once imagined the enormous amount of laundry produced by a family of nine. Do you have any idea how many pairs of socks a houseful of children and teenagers can go through in one week? I'll tell you, it's about a gazillion. Oh, and did I say pairs of socks? How silly of me! For mysterious reasons, our socks were always strictly mateless.

For a long time I took on the task of laundry all by myself. I could easily spend the entire day washing, drying, and folding load after load. I usually stood at the dining table to sort and fold, piling stacks of socks and undies from one end of the table to the other. By the time I had finished, the kids were usually home from school and off we'd race to baseball practice, Boy Scout meetings, and doctor's appointments. More often than not, when dinnertime rolled around, the table was still piled high with clean laundry.

On more occasions than I care to remember, dinner was eaten while standing in the dining room or scattered throughout the house. This was not what I wanted for my family. Eating together is an important tradition, and I decided that it was time for a change.

We tried many different strategies to effectively tackle the laundry problem, but nothing worked. Finally, in a stroke of sheer brilliance, I developed a routine that stuck. Each person was assigned a laundry day. It worked perfectly with seven kids for seven days.

Kids who were shorter than the washing machine were in charge of gathering their own dirty laundry and toting it to the laundry room where I would help them sort and wash it. Kids who were taller than the washing machine were required to do their own laundry. If they didn't clean their clothes, they might not have much to wear!

Our laundry system was a huge success. The kids learned how to wash their own clothes, we were able to sit down at the table to eat dinner, and, best of all, my marathon days of doing laundry disappeared forever!

MATERIALS

QUILT SIZE
60" x 72"

BLOCK SIZE
12½" unfinished, 12" finished

QUILT TOP
1 roll of 2½" print strips
1 yard background fabric
   – includes inner border

OUTER BORDER
1¼ yards – includes fabric for
   (2) 2½" strips

BINDING
¾ yard

BACKING
3¾ yards - horizontal seam(s)

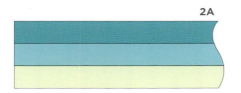

2A

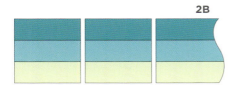

2B

3A

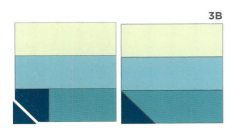

3B

3C

1 cut

From the background fabric, cut (5) 2½" strips across the width of the fabric. Subcut the strips into 2½" squares. Each strip will yield 16 squares and you need a **total of 80** squares. Set the remaining background fabric aside for the inner border.

From the outer border fabric, cut (2) 2½" strips across the width of the fabric. Mix these 2 strips in with the strips in the roll as you make strip sets. Set the remaining fabric aside for the outer border.

2 make strip sets

Sew (3) 2½" strips together along the length. Press all of the seam allowances in the same direction. **Make 14. 2A**

Cut the strip sets into 6½" squares. Each strip set will yield 6 squares and you need a **total of 80** squares. **2B**

3 block construction

Fold a 2½" background square once on the diagonal and press the crease in place. The crease will mark your sewing line. Repeat for all of the 2½" background squares. **3A**

Place a 2½" background square on the upper left corner of a 6½" strip set square, with right sides facing. Sew on the crease, then trim ¼" away from the sewn seam. Repeat for the remaining 6½" squares. **Make 80** units. **3B**

Sew 4 units together as shown. Notice the background triangles form a diamond where they meet in the center. **Make 20** blocks. **3C**

Block Size: 12½" unfinished, 12" finished

4 arrange & sew

Arrange the blocks in **5 rows** with each row made up of **4 blocks.** When you are happy with your arrangement, sew the blocks together into rows. Press the odd-numbered rows toward the left and the even-numbered rows toward the right. Nest the seams and sew the rows together.

5 inner border

Cut (6) 2½" strips across the width of the fabric. Sew the strips together end-to-end to make 1 long strip. Trim the inner borders from this strip.

Measure, cut, and attach the inner borders. The strips are approximately 60½" for the sides and approximately 52½" for the top and bottom.

6 outer border

Cut (7) 4½" strips across the width of the fabric. Sew the strips together end-to-end to make 1 long strip. Trim the outer borders from this strip.

Measure, cut, and attach the outer borders. The strips are approximately 64½" for the sides and approximately 60½" for the top and bottom.

7 quilt & bind

See pages 18-25 for tips on finishing your quilt!

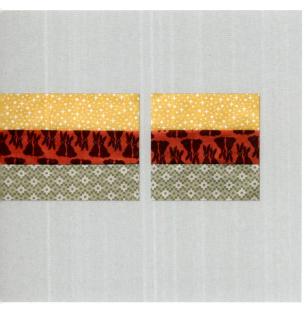

1 Sew (3) 2½" strips together. Cut the strip sets into 6½" squares.

2 Fold and place a 2½" square on 1 corner of a 6½" strip-pieced square. Sew in place using the crease as your stitching line.

3 Trim the excess fabric away ¼" from the sewn seam.

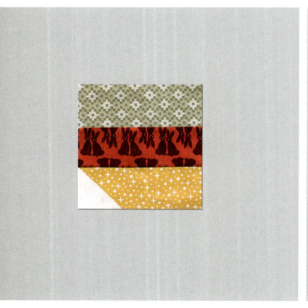

4 Open and press the seam allowance toward the corner triangle.

5 Arrange 4 squares so that the corner triangles meet in the center, as shown. Sew the squares together in pairs to form rows. Press the seams in opposite directions.

6 Nest the seams and sew the rows together. Press the seam in 1 direction to complete the block.

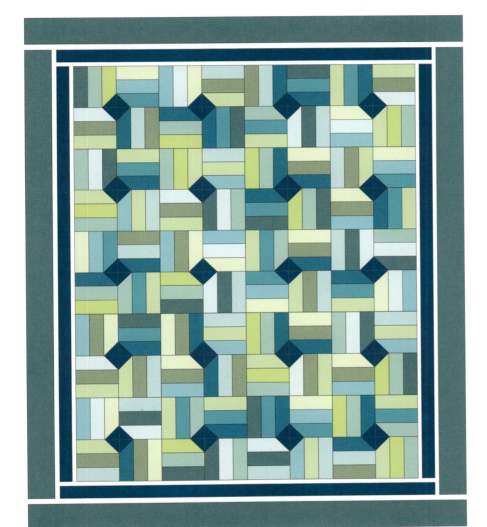

TEA TOWEL APRON

Tea for two, and two for tea. This easy tea towel apron is cute as can be! Some tea towels are just too darling to use for drying dishes. Don't hide your dish towel away in a drawer, use it to create an apron with handy pockets at the top and bottom accented by a row of sweet ruffles along the hemline.It really couldn't be simpler. The shape of the apron is created by trimming the top corners of a tea towel and adding single tie that threads through the top and sides. You can accessorize it with pockets wherever you like them best and even add a decorative button for extra appeal.

MATERIALS

PROJECT SIZE
18" x 28"

PROJECT SUPPLIES
1 tea towel (approximately 18" x 28")
(2-3) 2½" strips for apron tie

OPTIONAL
¼ yard coordinating fabric
    for a large pocket
(2-3) 2½" strips for ruffles
(2) 5" coordinating squares
    for mini pockets
1 small button

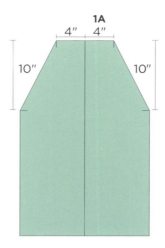

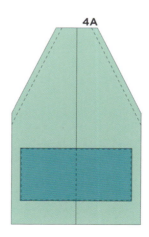

1 shape apron

Fold the towel in half lengthwise and press to crease. Reopen the towel and smooth it out. Measure 4" from the center fold along the top edge and make a mark. On the same side of the fold, measure 10" down from the top along the edge of the towel and mark that point. Make a fold connecting the 2 marks and press to crease. Measure and cut 1" away from the fold line. Repeat for the opposite side so you have now removed the top 2 corners of the towel. **1A**

2 make casing

Turn the raw edges of the cut corners of the apron under ¼" with wrong sides touching. Press. Turn the folded edges under ¾" to enclose the raw edges. Press. Topstitch to finish the casing. **2A**

3 make apron tie

Use (2-3) 2½" strips for the apron tie. Remove any selvages and piece the strips together with diagonal seams. Press the seams open.

Fold the short ends of the strip in ½" with wrong sides together. Press the strip in half lengthwise, wrong sides together. Reopen the strip and then fold each long raw edge in to meet at the center crease, wrong sides together. Refold the first fold capturing both sides. Topstitch around the entire apron tie.

Thread 1 end of the tie through 1 casing and down through the other, creating a neck loop at the top.

4 optional large pocket

From the coordinating fabric you chose for the large pocket, cut an 8" strip across the width of the fabric. Subcut (2) 8" x 16" rectangles.

Lay 1 rectangle on top of the other, right sides together. Sew around the perimeter of the stacked rectangles with a ¼" seam allowance. Be sure to backstitch at the beginning and end of your seam and leave a 4" opening along the bottom edge.

Clip the corners and turn the pocket right side out. Tuck the raw edges inside the opening and press the pocket flat. Topstitch along the top about ⅛" from the edge.

Fold the pocket in half and finger press along the center of the pocket. Line up the center fold of the pocket with the center fold of the apron, placing it as high or low on the apron as you like. Pin the pocket in place and then topstitch about ⅛" from the edge along the sides and bottom of the pocket, backstitching at each end. Notice that the opening you used for turning will be closed by this seam line. Topstitch down the center fold of the apron, backstitching at each end, to form 2 sections in the pocket. **4A**

5 optional raw-edged ruffle

Sew a long basting stitch ¼" along the length of (1) 2½" strip. Pull the bobbin thread to gather the ruffle. Pin the ruffled strip in place on the apron. Each ruffle should be placed about 2" up from the bottom of the apron and then spaced about every 2" from there. Adjust the ruffles evenly across the apron and then stitch it in place on top of the basting stitch, backstitching at each end. Add as many or as few ruffles as you like!

6 optional mini pocket

Lay (1) 5" square on top of the other, right sides together. Sew around the perimeter of the stacked squares with a ¼" seam allowance. Be sure to backstitch at the beginning and end of your seam and leave a small opening along the bottom edge.

Clip the corners and turn the pocket right side out. Tuck the raw edges inside the opening and press the pocket flat. Make a mark 2" from a corner along both adjacent edges of the square. Topstitch along the corner about ⅛" from the edge. **6A**

Make a fold connecting your 2 marks and press. **6B**

We added a small button to our pocket. If you'd like to do the same, you can add the button to the apron and a button hole to the mini pocket before attaching it to the apron.

Finger press the mini pocket in half and place it along the center fold of the apron as low or as high as you like. **6C**

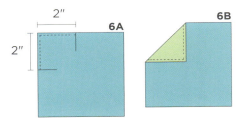

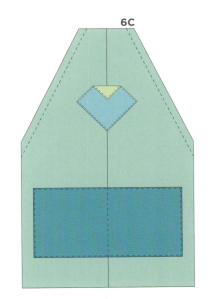

Journal

Journaling can be a great way to gain insight about yourself as a quilter and as a person. These prompts below are here to help you think more deeply about the way you like to learn. Then, you can take your new skills and apply them to your next project!

1 ARE YOU A STARTER AND ENJOY THE PROCESS OF BEGINNING A NEW PROJECT? OR ARE YOU A FINISHER AND MORE INTERESTED IN COMPLETING A PROJECT?
Knowing the part of quilting you enjoy most can help you focus your energy towards that part.

2 HAVE YOU EXPLORED A NEW TECHNIQUE LATELY?
Learning new skills helps us to become better quilters. What are three things you'd like to learn more about?

3 WHAT IS ONE THING YOU LEARNED FROM YOUR LAST QUILTING PROJECT?

Quilt Planner

Start your next quilt project with a plan and you'll be amazed at the results! As you begin with the end in mind, you'll be able to be more flexible as your project progresses and let go of the idea of perfection. After all, finished is better than perfect!

PROJECT IDEA _____

_____

_____

FABRICS _____

_____

COLORS

PRECUTS USED _____

_____

_____

YARDAGE _____

BLOCK DESIGN

SIZE _____ **X** _____

SKETCH   _SIZE_ _____ **X** _____

NOTES _____

_____

_____

_____

_____

_____

_____

_____

Build Your Own

Use this space to sketch or draw your own design based on the patterns in this section.

DISAPPEARING HOURGLASS 2   32

QUILT SIZE
79" x 90"

BLOCK SIZE
11½" unfinished, 11" finished

QUILT TOP
1 package 10" print squares
1 package 10" background squares

INNER BORDER
¾ yard

OUTER BORDER
1¼ yards

BINDING
¾ yard

BACKING
8¼ yards - vertical seam(s)
   or 2¾ yards 108" wide

DRUNKARD'S DOTS   44

QUILT SIZE
73" x 73"

BLOCK SIZE
10" unfinished, 9½" finished

QUILT TOP
1 package of 10" print squares
1 package of 10" background squares

INNER BORDER
½ yard

MIDDLE BORDER
½ yard

OUTER BORDER
1¼ yards

BINDING
¾ yard

BACKING
4½ yards – vertical seam(s)
   or 2¼ yards of 108" wide

ADDITIONAL SUPPLIES
Missouri Star Drunkard's Path Circle
   Template Set - Large
Missouri Star Drunkard's Path Circle
   Template Set - Small

50   GRAND ADVENTURES

QUILT SIZE
90¾" x 87¾"

BLOCK SIZE
15½" x 18½" unfinished,
15" x 18" finished

QUILT TOP
1 package of 10" print squares
1 package of 10" background squares

INNER BORDER
¾ yard

OUTER BORDER
1¾ yards

BINDING
1 yard

BACKING
8 yards - vertical seam(s)
  or 2¾ yards 108" wide

56   JUMP RINGS

QUILT SIZE
66" x 81½"

BLOCK SIZE
9" x 10" unfinished,
8½" x 9½" finished

QUILT TOP
1 package 10" print squares
2¼ yards background fabric
  - includes inner border

OUTER BORDER
1¼ yards

BINDING
¾ yard

BACKING
5 yards - vertical seam(s)
  or 2½ yards 108" wide

TOTALLY TULIPS 62

QUILT SIZE
89" x 90"

BLOCK SIZE
9½" x 17½" unfinished,
9" x 17" finished

QUILT TOP
1 package 10" print squares
¼ yard solid - tulip stems
3¾ yards background fabric
  - includes inner border

OUTER BORDER
1½ yards

BINDING
¾ yard

BACKING
7 yards - vertical seam(s)
  or 2¾ yards of 108" wide

IRISH CHANGE 68

QUILT SIZE
100½" x 100½"

BLOCK SIZE
10" unfinished, 9½" finished

QUILT TOP
1 package 10" print squares
1½ yards accent fabric
3¼ yards background fabric
  - includes inner border

OUTER BORDER
1¾ yards

BINDING
1 yard

BACKING
9¼ yards - vertical seam(s)
  or 3¼ yards 108" wide

74   DISAPPEARING PINWHEEEL ARROW

QUILT SIZE
81" x 92"

BLOCK SIZE
11½" unfinished, 11" finished

QUILT TOP
1 package 10" print squares
1 package of 10" background squares

INNER BORDER
¾ yard

OUTER BORDER
1¾ yards

BINDING
¾ yard

BACKING
7½ yards – horizontal seam(s)

80   LATTICE ARROWS

QUILT SIZE
88" x 88"

BLOCK SIZE
9½" unfinished, 9" finished

QUILT TOP
1 package 10" print squares
4½ yards dark blue fabric
   - includes outer border
2½ yards green fabric
1¼ yards white solid
   - includes inner border

BINDING
¾ yard

BACKING
8 yards – vertical seam(s)
   or 2¾ yards of 108" wide

PRAIRIE FLOWER 86

QUILT SIZE
74" x 89½"

BLOCK SIZE
14" unfinished, 13½" finished

QUILT TOP
1 package 10" squares
3¼ yards background fabric
  - includes sashing and inner border
¼ yard for cornerstones

OUTER BORDER
1½ yards

BINDING
¾ yard

BACKING
5½ yards - vertical seam(s) or
  2¾ yards 108" wide

FALL SHENANIGANS 92

WALL HANGING SIZE
40½" x 40"

SUPPLIES
1 package 10" print squares
  (we used Halloween-themed fabric)
½ yard background fabric

BORDER
½ yard

BINDING
½ yard

BACKING
2⅔ yards - vertical seam(s)

OTHER
(1) 4½" x 6½" Heat 'n Bond Lite
Missouri Star Large Simple Wedge
  Template for 10" Squares

CUTE CAMPER PILLOW 100

PROJECT SIZE
Fits a 16" pillow form

BLOCK SIZE
12½" unfinished, 12" finished

PILLOW TOP
1 package 10" print squares
½ yard background fabric

PILLOW BACK
¾ yard

OTHER
(1) ¼" diameter button
(1) ¾" - 1" diameter button
(1) 14" zipper
½ yard Heat n Bond Lite
18" square batting

116   DIZZY DAISY

QUILT SIZE
79" x 90"

BLOCK SIZE
9½" unfinished, 9" finished

QUILT TOP
4 matching packages of
   5" print squares
4¼ yards background fabric
   – includes inner border

OUTER BORDER
1¾ yards - includes cornerstones

BINDING
¾ yard

BACKING
5½ yards - vertical seam(s)
   or 2¾ yards 108" wide

122   FALLING CHARMS

QUILT SIZE
82" x 95"

BLOCK SIZE
7" unfinished, 6½" finished

QUILT TOP
4 packages of 5" squares
1 roll of 2½" background strips
   (42" width of fabric)
1½ yards 42" wide matching
   background fabric - includes border

BINDING
¾ yard

BACKING
8½ yards - vertcial seam(s)
   or 3 yards 108" wide

LUCKY PENNY   132

QUILT SIZE
45½" x 57"

QUILT TOP
2 packages 5" print squares
2 packages 5" background squares

BORDER
½ yard

BINDING
½ yard

BACKING
3 yards - horizontal seam(s)

OTHER
Missouri Star Small
  Half-Hexagon Template for
  5" squares & 2½" strips

PERIWINKLE   138

QUILT SIZE
58" x 70"

BLOCK SIZE
12½" unfinished, 12" finished

QUILT TOP
2 packages 5" print squares
3¾ yards background fabric

BORDER
1 yard

BINDING
¾ yard

BACKING
3¾ yards - horizontal seam(s)

ADDITIONAL SUPPLIES
1 package Mini Wacky Web
  Triangle Paper Refills
Missouri Star Small Half Hexagon
  Template for 5" Charm Packs
  & 2½" Jelly Rolls
Glue Stick - optional

144   HAPPY LITTLE HOUSES

QUILT SIZE
56" x 65"

BLOCK SIZE
4½" x 10½" unfinished,
4" x 10" finished

QUILT TOP
3 packages 5" print squares
½ yard navy solid fabric
2¼ yards light blue solid fabric
   - includes blue sashing

SASHING
¾ yard coordinating green
   print fabric

BINDING
¾ yard

BACKING
3½ yards - horizontal seam(s)

152   JACOB'S LADDER

QUILT SIZE
72" x 76"

BLOCK SIZE
4½" unfinished, 4" finished

QUILT TOP
5 packages of 5" light squares
5 packages of 5" dark squares

BINDING
¾ yard

BACKING
4¾ yards - vertical seam(s)
   or 2½ yards of 108" wide

ALL MY LOVE   162

QUILT SIZE
31½" x 31½"

BLOCK SIZE
9½" unfinished, 9" finished

QUILT TOP
3 packages 2½" print squares*
½ yard background fabric
   - includes sashing

BORDER
¾ yard

BINDING
½ yard

BACKING
1¼ yards

*__Note:__ You can replace the 3 packages of 2½"
print squares with 1 package of 5" print squares.
Simply cut the 5" squares in half both vertically
and horizontally to yield 2½" squares before
beginning the pattern._

HALF-SQUARE HARMONY BAG   168

PROJECT SIZE
16" x 20"

BLOCK SIZE
4½" unfinished, 4" finished

PROJECT SUPPLIES
1 package 5" print squares
1 yard coordinating print
   - includes strap & lining
25½" x 40" scrap of batting

HALF-HEXI SNOWMAN   174

QUILT SIZE
19" X 45"

TABLE RUNNER TOP
9 _pairs_ of matching 5" print squares
(1) 5" dark print square
1 scrap of black for buttons, mouths,
   and eyes - approximately 4" x 7"
1 scrap of orange for noses
   - approximately 2" x 3"
½ yard white solid

SASHING, BORDER, & BINDING
¾ yard dark print

OTHER
2½" x 17" rectangle of fusible web
Missouri Star Large Half-Hexagon
   Template for 10" Squares

BACKING
1½ yards

188 DESERT SUNSET

QUILT SIZE
59" x 59"

BLOCK SIZE
13½" unfinished, 13" finished

QUILT TOP
1 roll of 2½" x 42" strips

BORDER
¾ yard

BINDING
½ yard

BACKING
3¾ yards – vertical seam(s)

194 BINDING TOOL STAR

QUILT SIZE
77" x 77"

BLOCK SIZE
16½" unfinished, 16" finished

QUILT TOP
1 roll 2½" print strips
2¾ yards background fabric
 - includes inner border

PIANO KEY BORDER
1 package 5" print squares

BINDING
¾ yard

BACKING
4¾ yards – vertical seam(s)
 or 2½ yards 108" wide

OTHER
The Binding Tool By TQM Products

JELLY ROLL RACE 3   204

QUILT SIZE
66½" x 79"

QUILT TOP
1 roll of 2½" print strips
1 yard background fabric
  - includes inner border

OUTER BORDER
1¼ yards

BINDING
¾ yard

BACKING
5 yards – vertical seam(s)
  or 2½ yards 108" wide

PIECE OUT   210

QUILT SIZE
60" x 72"

BLOCK SIZE
12½" unfinished, 12" finished

QUILT TOP
1 roll of 2½" print strips
1 yard background fabric
  – includes inner border

OUTER BORDER
1¼ yards – includes fabric for
  (2) 2½" strips

BINDING
¾ yard

BACKING
3¾ yards - horizontal seam(s)

216 TEA TOWEL APRON

PROJECT SIZE
18" x 28"

PROJECT SUPPLIES
1 tea towel (approximately 18" x 28")
(2-3) 2½" strips for apron tie

OPTIONAL
¼ yard coordinating fabric
  for a large pocket
(2-3) 2½" strips for ruffles
(2) 5" coordinating squares
  for mini pockets
1 small button

ARTICLES

ACKNOWLEDGMENTS

From the beginning, Block has been a work of heart. We started out with such a small team including my two children, Natalie Earnheart and Al Doan, along with our Creative Director, Christine Ricks, and a pattern writer. I helped sew the quilts with Natalie and we even created the visual directions to sew each block, step by step, all on our own. It was quite a challenge and I am so grateful for the wonderful team who brought Block to life. Nowadays, over 20 people bring their skills and talents together to publish Block. I want to thank our dedicated team for all their hard work over the years and their commitment to making Block the very best it can be!

The Block team is a well-oiled machine and I want to thank my daughter, Natalie, for all she does as the Executive Editor. She's my right-hand girl and together we're able to come up with so many fun ideas! I want to thank our hard-working Creative Director, Christine Ricks, for her tireless efforts to make each issue attractive, interesting, and easy to read. Her direction over the years has been phenomenal. I want to thank our pattern writers who take our quilts and create detailed patterns to go along with them. I know it's not always easy to interpret these designs and I'm grateful for their patience! I want to thank our sewists who work to remake each quilt from scratch and do such a great job. They make it look easy and I can't imagine doing this without them. I want to thank our writers who take our stories and our customers' stories and give them the care and attention they deserve. I want to thank our photographers who take lovely photographs to accompany each article and make us all look so good! And I want to thank our printing coordinator who keeps us on track and gets Block in the mail on time.

A big thanks goes out to my husband, Ron, for always supporting me and lugging around so many quilts! He's even become a quilter in his own right and I love the designs he creates. I want to thank my children for their willingness to tell stories, share, and appear in so many photoshoots! I have seen my cute grandchildren grow up in the pages of Block and it warms my heart.

Finally, I want to thank you, all the quilters who have supported Missouri Star over the years and have read and subscribed to Block. We couldn't do it without you!